UNITED STATES NAVY MEMORIAL

*A
Living
Tradition*

★ ★ ★ *Special Plankowner Edition* ★ ★ ★

UNITED STATES NAVY MEMORIAL

A Living Tradition

John W. Alexander
Commander, U.S. Navy
Editor and Producer

THE UNITED STATES NAVY MEMORIAL FOUNDATION was formed in 1977 by naval and civic leaders who shared the goal of both honoring our Navy and its significant contributions to "America's origin, development and survival" and promoting an awareness that ours is a "maritime nation, born of the sea, and dependent on the seas for its security and commerce." These quotations from retired Rear Admiral William Thompson, President of the Foundation, express the strong feelings that motivated these leaders: former Chairman of the Joint Chiefs of Staff Thomas H. Moorer; former Chief of Naval Operations Admiral Arleigh A. Burke; and former Secretaries of the Navy J. William Middendorf II and John W. Warner. It was they who organized and incorporated the organization and secured the approval of the governmental agencies whose consent was essential.

Sponsored solely by tax-deductible contributions (IRS 501 (C)3), the United States Navy Memorial Foundation is a non-profit organization.

Published by the United States Navy Memorial Foundation. Profits from the sale of this book will be used to defray the cost of construction and maintenance of the Memorial.

© 1987 United States Navy Memorial Foundation
All rights reserved.
ISBN 0-9619812-0-2
Printed in the United States of America

FIRST EDITION

Book Design: Ernest McIver

Illustrations: Susan G. Gamble

Photo Editor: Russell Egnor

Research Assistant: Judy VanBenthuysen

Typography: Pica and Points

Printing and Color Separations: Stephenson inc

Editorial Board

*F*or my father, John S. Alexander, a quartermaster assigned to PT boats in the Philippines during World War II; my father-in-law, Richard Pietropaoli, who served as a Lieutenant Junior Grade aboard a surface combatant out of New London, Connecticut, in World War II; my brother-in-law, Ronald H. Zucker, who served as a second class electronics technician for four years aboard Atlantic Fleet destroyers; my brother-in-law, Lieutenant Commander Stephen Pietropaoli, a Surface Warfare qualified public affairs officer still on active duty in the Navy; my wife, Theresa Marie, who served as a Lieutenant Junior Grade Navy nurse; and finally, to all lone sailors past and present, whose dedication, sacrifice, commitment and professionalism have served to defend, protect and uphold our country's freedom.

This book is also dedicated to the more than 50 photographers and artists whose photographic excellence, artistic skill and creative imagination made putting this volume together such an enjoyable challenge.

Navy's hot air balloon during the Albuquerque International Balloon Festival.

Commissioning, Enlistment and Reenlistment Oath

"I do solemnly swear that I will support and defend the Constitution of
the United States of America against all enemies, foreign and domestic;
that I will bear true faith and allegiance to the same; that I will obey the
orders of the President of the United States and the orders of the officers
appointed over me; and that I will take this obligation freely, without
any mental reservation or purpose of evasion. So help me God."

At A Glance

For Invaluable Assistance

NORMALLY, ACKNOWLEDGEMENTS are to those who helped an author in the preparation of a book. However, because of the nature of this commemorative publication, on this page we recognize a few individuals for their assistance in planning, designing, building and funding the United States Navy Memorial.

It was necessary that many individuals participate in this venture to build a major national memorial, especially in a city replete with memorials and in a city which is the ultimate in the good and bad of bureaucratic processes.

To begin, for two years Mrs. Ruth Donohue was my only assistant and it was she who first mentioned the subject of an amphitheater for all the military bands to use. This embryonic jewel grew into a concept which persisted and dominated our thinking to become the primary reason the U.S. Navy Memorial Foundation gained access to the prestigious site at Market Square on Pennsylvania Avenue.

Captain Walter "R" Thomas worked with us for three years until he retired to write a book which he "had to get out" of his head. It was he, Navy artist John Charles Roach, Navy Memorial Sculptor Stanley Bleifeld and me who conceptualized and developed a rough design of the Memorial and turned it over to the good hands of our architect, Conklin Rossant of New York City, for fine tuning and engineering drawings. Peter Mahoney was the principal with Conklin Rossant.

Captain Bob Jones, an experienced administrator with a 20 megabyte memory and a penchant for work, was the "nuts and bolts guy" for the past three years as an outstanding Executive Assistant.

Although the staff was small in proportion to the task (never more than ten, including part timers and an occasional "temporary"), it performed well as a team and didn't stray off course to the primary objective of building a Memorial. Those loyal, hard working staff personalities, who will remain forever in my fondest memories, are covered in detail in the article on the history of the Memorial.

Tom Regan, a former Civil Engineer Naval officer and Executive Director of the Pennsylvania Avenue Development Corporation, provided the counsel necessary to guide us through the real and imaginary mine fields of Washington bureaucracy. Max Berry and Henry Berliner, former and present Chairmen of the

PADC, encouraged us to persevere inspite of adversities.

A prestigious, energetic board of directors is important to an ambitious undertaking such as this. Early on, it was decided that the prestigious aspect of our board far outweighed the energetic part, so my "young turks" were installed as members—S. Steven Karalekas, a successful young lawyer; B. Waring Partridge, an enterprising management consultant and William S. Norman, Executive Vice President of AMTRAK. Tom Regan was added later and these became the "heavy duty" functionaries of the board, with "Spike" Karalekas serving as General Counsel and a participant in most decisions. Retired Admiral Thomas H. Moorer and Edward Hidalgo were especially helpful in fund raising.

We had many who volunteered to help and some who did. Special praise is necessary for the lead volunteer for her hard work and long hours, at times on menial, but "somebody had to do it" tasks, my wife, Dorothy Thompson. It should be said that the entire Thompson family was involved in the Memorial. Our two sons,Craig and Brian, worked at various times; our daughter, Stevii Graves, is a part-timer on the staff, mothering the office computers, and is Navy Memorial Log coordinator; her two teenagers, Stefanie and Will, were involved at times, and even eight-year old Braden would appear to "help the girls in the office."

Public Law 96-199 which authorized the Foundation to build the Navy Memorial stipulated that no federal or District of Columbia monies could be used to fund construction, only donations from the private sector. Thus, fund raising was an important and time consuming factor. All contributors to the Memorial are acknowledged for their support of the project but because of timing or other circumstances, several deserve special mention: Foundation Director Joanne Crown of Chicago was responsible for a gift of $50,000 from the Crown Foundation in 1979 which kept us afloat for several months; Thomas H. Pownall, Chairman, Martin Marietta Corp., for the first significant corporate contribution; H. Ross Perot's one million dollar line of credit permitted us to commence construction, guaranteeing total funding for the first phase of the Memorial; G.E.R. "Gus" Kinnear, who encouraged Grumman Corporation to make the largest corporate gift of $250,000, and to National President William McCarley, Executive Secretary Robert Nolan and the Fleet Reserve Association for the pledge of $1,000,000 which exemplified and amplified the outstanding support received from Navy enlisted personnel.

A bow to Jay Brodie and his PADC staff; George White, Architect of the Capitol and Chairman of the PADC Design Committee; Reg Griffith and his National Capital Planning Commission staff; J. Carter Brown and Charles Atherton of the Commission of Fine Arts and Jack Fish and John Parsons of the National Park Service, Capital Region. Also, special gratitude to Gilbane-Jackson, Inc., and to contractors W. M. Slosser, Inc., Pagliaro Brothers Stone Co. and New England Stone Industries, Inc. who didn't just show up for work each day—they were there "to build a Memorial."

On behalf of the ten-and-a-half million men and women who have served in the United States Navy, and who were the inspiration for this endeavor, we extend our appreciation to the above and many more who have made this "Living Memorial" a major addition to our Nation's beautiful capital city.

William Thompson
Rear Admiral, U.S. Navy (Retired)
President, U.S. Navy Memorial Foundation

Indian Ocean . . . an officer aboard the frigate *USS Badger* measures distance to another ship of the formation with a Fisk-type stadimeter.

"American sailors have etched an indelible record of courage in the logbook of liberty."

THIS LIVING MEMORIAL is a proud and stirring tribute to the men and women of the United States Navy who have served and will continue to serve our country, in peace and war, with gallantry and devotion. It is a remarkable addition to the landscape of our Capital City, a means, in the words of Pierre L'Enfant who first proposed the erection of such a monument, "to consecrate" the Navy's "progress and achievements."

From its founding in 1775 to its current strength of nearly 600 ships, the United States Navy has been a bulwark of America's security and a shield of safe passage in international waters. Its history is one of uncommon valor in the cause of freedom and of unswerving dedication to the cherished principles that have made America great. Through "the perilous fight" of wartime and the watchful nights of peacetime, American sailors have etched an indelible record of courage in the logbook of liberty. The names of some of the greatest among them evoke the greatness that belongs to them all: John Paul Jones, Stephen Decatur, Chester Nimitz, William Halsey. It is altogether fitting that, on this wide avenue that has been so many solemn marches and joyous parades, a grateful Nation should erect a permanent sign of loving tribute.

In its granite grid and open space, its bronze sculptures and mast-like colonnades, its fountains and waterfalls, the Navy Memorial captures the variety and mystery of the great oceans, the very qualities which have attracted men and women to serve at sea for more than 200 years. The Lone Sailor, in his rough peacoat, with his unturned collar and confident gaze that forever seeks the horizon, symbolizes the patience and resolve that are the essence of America's maritime spirit.

Teddy Roosevelt called our Navy the "right arm of the United States of America" and a "peacemaker." We can rejoice that through the centuries it has been both, and we ask God's continued blessings on this land and on all who defend it under, on, and above the sea.

Nancy joins me in sending best wishes to all of you.

HERE AT LAST IS A LIVING MEMORIAL which honors the men and women of the Navy—past, present and future. To these dedicated Americans falls the endless and difficult task of defending the precious liberty and democracy which our ancestors proclaimed in documents now enshrined in the National Archives, across the street from the Navy Memorial.

American sailors have maintained the watch, 24 hours a day, 365 days a year, since the founding of our country. Individually, their deeds rarely match the nation's glory for which they are performed—the cold, storm-drenched midwatches at sea; lonely vigils worlds away from home; exhaustion from round-the-clock at battle stations; torn from families and loved-ones while the rest of the world pays little mind. But taken together, the good works of Navy people are nothing less than heroic, whether in peacetime or war, whether at home, on foreign shores or the seven seas.

In this bicentennial year of the Constitution, we celebrate America's most cherished ideal—freedom for all people. In the Navy Memorial, we honor the patriots, heroes and everyday people of the Navy who, through personal sacrifice and devotion to duty, help freedom prevail.

The Honorable John G. Tower
Master Chief Boatswain's Mate, USNR
Chairman, U.S. Navy Memorial Foundation

I CAN THINK OF NO FINER TRIBUTE to those men and women who have served our country at sea, in war and in peace, than to dedicate this superb memorial. Upon completion, it will tell the seagoing story of a maritime nation. From our birth as a nation, we have depended on the ability to sail the seas in peace. Out of this need our Navy was born, and its purpose to this day is still to allow freedom of transit at sea. That task has not always been easy. Our sailors and marines have, however, met every challenge before them, whether it be in Tripoli Harbor in 1803 or the Persian Gulf in 1987.

As a former naval officer, this memorial holds special significance for me. I learned much from the Navy during my days as a young pilot who served during World War II.

Few memorials could be as appropriate as this one. Its design merges past and present and looks to the future, as the lone sailor staring at the sea. It merges the individual and the world, as the sailor views a world spreading out around him. It merges peace and war, for the memorial pays tribute to the navies of other nations in a spirit of community and not conflict. Finally, this living memorial celebrates life, not death, for it is a gathering place, a place to enjoy the company of others and to learn of our nation's past.

So, as an American and a serviceman, I congratulate all who have made this living memorial a reality.

The Honorable George Bush
Vice President of the United States

Dedication committee chairman John Cosgrove, below, and U.S. Navy
Memorial Foundation President Rear Admiral William Thompson,
U.S. Navy, (Ret.), introduce dignitaries in the audience and welcome
veterans and friends to the ceremony.

A Dedication Fit for the Navy

Tom Coldwell

The day was as sharp and bright as a diamond chandelier, the air fresh as full sails on a square-rigger. The pageantry, the grandeur of it all! It was trumpet fanfares and fireworks, choirs speaking our hearts and speakers singing praise, flags unfurling and blue and gold balloons lofting above the requisite pomp and considerable circumstance of a great Navy day.

This was the long awaited official dedication of the U.S. Navy Memorial, October 13, 1987, square in the middle of the 212th birthday of the United States Navy. The Navy brought out the big guns on the balcony of the National Archives across the street from the Memorial: the Secretary of the Navy, the Chief of Naval Operations, the Master Chief Petty Officer of the Navy. Nearly all of their living predecessors gathered in the audience. A far larger throng were Navy veterans from all over America—a pride of yesteryear's seagoing lions, bemedaled and hashmarked from here to liberty call, bringing their broad smiles and bright, sometimes glistening eyes to some special moments over the Tuesday noon hour when "their" Memorial came to life.

Shortly after 11:00 a.m., a crowd of 8,000 filtered into a rectangle of folding chairs set up on Pennsylvania Avenue—closed here for the day—between the National Archives on the south and the Memorial on the north. Four Navy bands, the U.S. Navy Concert Band and the Sea Chanters, the U.S. Navy Ceremonial Band, the U.S. Naval Academy Band and the combined U.S. Atlantic Fleet and Armed Forces School of Music Band took positions at each corner of the rectangle and played for 40 minutes while guests arrived and officials assembled.

As the overture neared an end, 92 veterans marched in carrying placards with the names of their ship and squadron reunion groups and Navy related associations. The march-on was simple and touching: these are the Memorial's people. Before the actual ceremony began,

Tom Coldwell, a retired Navy captain, is a public relations consultant and free lance writer.

Mrs. Jean Arthurs, president of the National Association of Military Widows, places a floral wreath at the top of the compass rose, left; a pageant of flags from all the states and U.S. territories; Chairman of the Joint Chiefs of Staff Admiral William J. Crowe, left, with Chief of Naval Operations Admiral Carlisle A.H. Trost; the Naval Air Training Command Choir.

"Bless Our Navy and All Who Love and Serve Her"

Dear God, whose Spirit was moving over the face of the waters in the beginning; we thank you for this day, and for those who have served you, their fellow man, and their nation in our Navy.

We offer special thanks for the people whose vision saw this day and this place, and who have contributed time, effort, inspiration and money, and who, by their presence here today, give of themselves.

We ask you to be present in all we do and say here today.

We ask your special blessing upon this National Navy Memorial. May it be a timeless and living reminder of dedicated service to our country in defense of freedom.

May what we dedicate here today help inspire and perpetuate the finest of Navy ideals: pride in an honorable profession, care and concern for others, perseverance in adversity, courage in danger, preservation of sacred honor, and trust in you our God.

Lord God, you know the many who have given much—including their very lives—that we may stand here today. Help us to do justice to their memory.

Help us also remember the families who wait at home for those who go down to the sea in ships.

Dear God and Father of us all, bless our Navy and all who love and serve her—this day and forevermore. Amen.

Reverend H. Burton Shepherd
Rear Admiral, U.S. Navy (Ret.)

Invocation given at the United States Navy Memorial Dedication, October 13, 1987.

there was a preamble, with Rear Admiral William Thompson, President of the Navy Memorial Foundation, introducing dignitaries in the audience and acknowledging all who "made it happen". Washington communications consultant and dedication committee chairman John Cosgrove set the tone for the ceremony; Henry A. Berliner, Jr., chairman of the Pennsylvania Avenue Development Corporation, noted with pride his corporation's partnership in the Memorial project.

Precisely at noon, the ceremony began, with former senior Senator from Texas and Naval Reserve Master Chief Bostswain's Mate, the Honorable John G. Tower, chairman of the board of the Navy Memorial Foundation, serving as master of ceremonies. The ceremony proceeded with the presentation of the Colors, National Anthem, invocation and Navy Hymn. There followed performances by the bands, a pageant of flags from all the states and U.S. territories, a precision drill by the Navy Ceremonial Guard Drill Team and brief addresses by Admiral William J. Crowe, Chairman of the Joint Chiefs of Staff; Admiral Carlisle A. H. Trost, Chief of Naval Operations,; former Commandant of the Marine Corps, General P. X. Kelly, representing former LTjg George Bush, now Vice President of the United States; and the principal speaker, the Honorable Caspar W. Weinberger, Secretary of Defense.

Former senior Senator and Naval Reserve Master Chief Boatswain's Mate John Tower, and Secretary of Defense Caspar Weinberger, above right, were two of the distinguished speakers; Musician First Class Susan M. Bender sang the National Anthem; water from the Seven Seas was poured into the Memorial's serene pools.

Secretary of the Navy James H. Webb, Jr., below, enlisted a special
Recruit Company of 90 new sailors; and reenlisted 22 petty officers.

Admiral Thompson, left, shares a congratulatory handshake with Stanley Bleifeld, sculptor of the Lone Sailor. At right, Master Chief Petty Officer of the Navy William Plackett steps lively with young Braden Graves and Admiral Thompson, after the three "unveil" the Lone Sailor.

Secretary Weinberger said the Memorial immortalizes the spirit, character and personality of the 212-year-old Navy and the millions of dedicated men and women who have served in it. The Memorial "enshrines in stone and metal the gratitude of a nation," he said. Then he commanded, "let this great Navy Memorial come alive!"

The assembled bands blared their fanfares and spine-tingling strains from "Victory at Sea" while Navy Ceremonial Guardsmen "charged" the Memorial's quiet pools with vials of water from the Seven Seas, taken on a recent round-the-world voyage of a Navy submarine. As if driven by the oceans' tumult, the still waters energized in an eruption of fountains. Two hundred flag bearers encircled the 100-foot diameter granite map of the world which forms the central plaza of the Memorial. More sailors hauled up the National Ensign and the Navy flag on the two masts at the front of the Memorial while signal flags flew on the halyards.

Twenty thousand helium balloons launched into the crackling blue sky, and the whole evolution culminated in an authoritative, eye-wincing salute of 21 bursts of aerial pyrotechnics.

When the smoke cleared and the balloons headed for the suburbs, Master Chief Petty Officer of the Navy William H. Plackett addressed the throng and formally introduced to America the Memorial's key sculpture, the Lone Sailor, the seven-foot tall symbol of everyone in the Navy—past, present and future.

Then at another position on the Memorial site, the compass rose imbedded in stone near the entrance, three women stepped forward to place a floral wreath—in memory of great sacrifices of Navy people and their loved ones. Rear Admiral Thompson introduced them to the crowd: Mrs. Jean Arthurs, whose late husband was a highly decorated naval aviator in World War II, Korea and Vietnam, is president of the National Association of Military Widows; Mrs. Ann Mills Griffiths, executive director of the National League of Families of American Prisoners and Missing in Southeast Asia; her brother, a

Leader of the Navy Ceremonial Guard Drill Team barks an order.

naval aviator, was listed as missing in action in 1966 over North Vietnam; Mrs. Evelyn Stocki, a Gold Star Mother whose Navy son was killed in Vietnam.

As the dedication ceremony neared an end, the Honorable James H. Webb, Jr., Secretary of the Navy, stressed the importance of people in the Navy. "We don't send a naval force into a crisis. We don't send ships. We send people." Keying on the people theme, the Secretary reenlisted 22 petty officers and enlisted a "Navy Memorial Special Recruit Company"—90 young men recruited by Navy Recruiting District Washington. And as Mr. Webb spoke of people, four two-man crews of people flew over the scene in an impressively tight formation of Navy F-14 Tomcat fighter aircraft. Secretary Webb concluded his remarks with a surprise for Rear Admiral Thompson, presenting the admiral the Navy's Distinguished Public Service Award, "for his unswerving dedication, tireless efforts, and superb leadership, which enabled the United States Navy Memorial to become a reality."

Senator Tower closed the proceedings and kicked off the grand finale, a massive musical and daytime fireworks extravaganza and parade of flags, all the while the Memorial's fountains gurgled a joy of life and adventure of the sea. And the veterans stood proud, pulses racing with memories of service and shipmates, the comradeship of the Navy.

Then it was over. Or was it? The crowd dispersed and work crews backed in their trucks to clear away chairs for a bristling Pennsylvania Avenue rush hour to come. Up off the street and on the Memorial plaza, a ceremony of sorts continued. People gathered near, but not too near, the Lone Sailor, most of them Navy people, the old salts and their families. One by one in an orderly hushed reverence they took turns standing by the Lone Sailor while someone else snapped a picture. There was no crowding or rush among them, strangers at first, now mutual friends through their love for the Sailor. Later on they left.

At the feet of the Lone Sailor lay a single rose. The day was done.

Admiral Thompson, above right, listened while Navy Secretary James H. Webb, Jr., read the Distinguished Public Service Award citation; Chief Equipment Operator Richard Hoffman, a 40-year Navy veteran, enjoyed the festivities. Opposite, top, Barbara Eden was one of the distinguished guests at a fund raising dinner held a few months before the Memorial dedication; bottom, President and Commander-in-Chief Ronald Reagan accepts a replica of the Lone Sailor from John Cosgrove, left, and Admiral Thompson.

Launching the Navy Memorial

Clarence Johnson

ONE OF THE QUESTIONS MOST ASKED of those involved with the Navy Memorial is, "How long has the project been in process?" One of the more spectacular replies, in keeping with the dedication of the project, is, "Oh, about 200 years."

It's true. In his presentation of a design of Washington, D.C., the capital of the new nation, Major Pierre L'Enfant proposed an "itinerary" column be erected to commemorate the good deeds of the Navy. Despite the fact the U.S. Navy was only about 15 years old, it, indeed, had moments of glory during the American Revolution. In those days, columns were the vogue, witness Trafalgar Square in London, the naval columns in Venice and in Rome. Another indication that L'Enfant knew what he was doing is that his column was only about six city blocks from Market Square, the site of today's U.S. Navy Memorial at Pennsylvania Avenue and Eighth Street. L'Enfant's commemorative work of art was planned for the waterfront at the foot of eighth Street.

One can rightfully say that it takes a while to get things done in Washington, and the idea for a Navy memorial was occasionally resuscitated, but it wasn't until the Spring of 1977 that Admiral Arleigh A. Burke, a retired Chief of Naval Operations (CNO), declared that . . ."We have talked long enough about a Navy memorial and it's time we did something about it." As always, when the good admiral spoke, many listened.

He made that statement in the presence of Admiral Thomas H. Moorer, another former CNO and

Chairman of the Joint Chiefs of staff, and others in a meeting at the Pentagon with Admiral James L. Holloway, III, then the Chief of Naval Operations.

The admirals decided that the time had come for action, and Admiral Holloway assigned the task to his Chief of Information, Rear Admiral David Cooney, an excellent organizer and planner. Cooney wrestled with the project for several months, and when he learned that government funds could not be used, he set about establishing an organization to design, build and fund a Navy Memorial. He wisely called for assistance from naval reservists, retired officers and other distinguished Navy alumni who shortly brought about the organization of the U.S. Navy Memorial Foundation.

Admiral Cooney had enlisted the help of Samuel W. Sax, a Chicago businessman and Naval Reserve commander, and Albert E. Jenner of the Chicago law firm of Jenner and Block. Together they incorporated the Foundation in the State of Illinois as an educational organization, authorized to receive and administer funds for charitable purposes under section 501(c)(3) of the IRS code. Founding directors were former Secretary of the Navy William Middendorf, chairman and president; Sax, vice chairman; Jenner, secretary; Robert Ferneau, treasurer; Admirals Burke and Moorer; former Secretary of the Navy, Senator John Warner and James Griffin, of San Francisco, the immediate past president of the Navy League of the United States. At a subsequent meeting, Rear Admiral John J. Bergen, USNR (Retired), of New York City, was elected as the ninth member of the board of directors.

After announcing its existence and purpose at a reception in the historic manse Decatur House, near the White House, the Foundation achieved little for several months. Good intentions far exceeded the reality of the

CLARENCE JOHNSON is a free lance writer who resides in northern Virginia. A Navy veteran, he's followed the U.S. Navy Memorial's development with interest from its infancy.

Chief of Naval Operations James D. Watkins joins former Secretaries of the Navy John Warner, John Lehman, J. William Middendorf and Edward Hidalgo in breaking ground for the Navy Memorial. Chairman of the Joint Chiefs of Staff Admiral William Crowe and William Leonard, former Foundation chairman, are also pictured.

Former Secretaries of the Navy, from left, W. Graham Claytor, Edward Hidalgo, Senator John Warner and J. William Middendorf, seen with Secretary of the Navy John Lehman at future site of Navy Memorial.

project. Talk of the considerable horsepower that could be generated to accomplish great feats in this type of endeavor was soon muted by the almost total lack of understanding of how to proceed. The Foundation had no plans on paper or otherwise, as to design, site, scope or scale of a Navy Memorial. Even fund raising had ceased and its checkbook carried a balance of a paltry $25,000.

In April of 1978, retired Rear Admiral William Thompson, Cooney's predecessor as Chief of Information and a public relations consultant in Washington, D.C., volunteered to assist in getting the project started. He admitted that he knew nothing about building a memorial in the nation's capital, or any other place, but his background gave him faith in the wealth of information available in Washington at the other end of a telephone. He enlisted the help of a young, enterprising former naval officer, B. Waring Partridge, who was associated with the management consulting firm of McKinsey and Company, Inc. Partridge arranged for McKinsey to do a mini-study on how to build a memorial in Washington, done in two weeks by an intern graduate student. The study put in perspective the various elements of the process and provided a plan of action which was later augmented and studded with milestones. Basically, five major elements were identified for the memorial program. They were:

▪ ENABLING LEGISLATION: Any memorial of this nature to be constructed on public land in Washington, D.C. has to be authorized by the U.S. Congress.

▪ DESIGN: Three agencies of the U.S. government are principals in the approval of the design of any memorial—the Commission of Fine Arts, the National Capital Planning Commission and the Secretary of the Interior.

▪ SITE SELECTION: The same three agencies are the principals involved in approving a site within the confines of the District of Columbia.

▪ FUND RAISING: Before construction can begin on a site within the District of Columbia, a guarantee of construction funds is necessary.

▪ CONSTRUCTION AND MAINTENANCE: Normally, when a memorial is built on public lands in the District of Columbia, construction is the responsibility of the sponsoring organization. Upon completion, maintenance is done by the Secretary of the Interior through the National Park Service.

With the McKinsey road map in hand, Bill Thompson started to chart a path through the Washington bureaucracy. He called upon another young, hard charging Navy alumnus, S. Steven Karalekas, a Naval Academy graduate, a former Navy public affairs officer still active in the Naval Reserve. He was rising fast to become one of Washington's most successful young lawyers.

Karalekas had worked in the White House during the

There could never have been a Navy Memorial groundbreaking without Admiral Thompson and his wife Dorothy.

These enlisted men and women give their support and illustrate that the U.S. Navy Memorial is for all hands.

Nixon administration and also had been employed in the U.S. Congress. He was ideal to help get the enabling legislation into and out of the Congress. He and Thompson were assured that there would be no difficulty getting Congressional approval, only that it would be time-consuming.

While identical bills were introduced in the House and the Senate, Thompson and Karalekas decided to concentrate their efforts on the Senate because there were fewer members and the House would go along with the senior legislative body when the measure was considered. Time proved to be an important factor because it ran out on them in 1978. Former Secretary of the Navy John Chafee of Rhode Island introduced legislation in the Senate and Representative Bob Wilson of San Diego, the ranking member of the House Armed Services Committee, introduced the bill in the lower chambers.

The bills were reintroduced in 1979 and carefully guided along a successful path so that in March of 1980, President Jimmy Carter, a former Navy lieutenant, signed Public Law 96-199, an omnibus bill for the Department of the Interior, which in part authorized the foundation to proceed with construction of the Navy Memorial on public land in the District of Columbia when funds were guaranteed. The law specifically stated that no federal or District of Columbia funds could be expended on the memorial. Thompson and Karalekas

put a big check mark alongside that major milestone.

Coincidental to the legislative work, Thompson was moving ahead on the design and site aspects of the project. By this time he had been made Executive Director and was devoting more time to foundation business. Although he flinched at accusations that 32 years in the Navy didn't teach him about volunteering for things, especially impossible tasks, he became more involved. He looked on the project as an opportunity to make an expression about the Navy that would be much more monumental than anything he had done during a successful career as a naval officer.

He determined in the early stages that the Memorial had to be functional, and if a decent site were to be obtained, the concept would have to be appealing to all in the bureaucratic process. Desirable sites were fast disappearing and cost of land was intimidating. Funding for the memorial was sparse because few would back a high risk item, especially with no site, no design. The paucity of funds dictated the hiring of staff support.

In the early years, his only staff support was a loyal secretary, Mrs. Ruth Donohue, who for 20 years was the secretary to the Navy's Chief of Information. She returned to work when Thompson retired from the Navy and beckoned. Thompson credits Ruth Donohue for initiating the idea of centering the memorial on a concert stage to be used by all the area's military bands. This concept proved to be basic to all future plans for the memorial.

For some, military music connotes memories of a group of sailors or GI's getting together with musical instruments procured from almost anywhere to have a "session." They all started a tune together, but if they finished in unison, it was an event. However, the principal bands of the military service are talented groups with most members possessing bachelor or master degrees in music. When not on tour throughout the country and beyond, they play concerts in the Washington metropolitan area. Prior to 1973, the bands of the Army, Navy, Marine Corps and Air Force performed on the Watergate Barge which was moored near the Lincoln Memorial. This was popular venue for citizens in the area as well as tourists. However, Hurricane Agnes tore the barge from its moorings and moved it several miles down the Potomac River where it disintegrated.

The bands were disbursed to the Jefferson Memorial, Sylvan Theater and steps of the Capitol. It was not practical to replace the barge because aircraft operating out of Washington's National Airport would be flying through the music every minute or so. To provide an amphitheater for the military bands in Washington filled a long standing need. That became the basic premise of the Foundation strategy.

Early on, the Foundation touched base with the National Capital Planning Commission (NCPC) which indirectly proved quite helpful. Robert Brett, a retired Navy captain who had served his last four tours of duty as a public affairs specialist with Admiral Tom Moorer, a foundation founder, joined Thompson in some early calls. Brett had joined the Washington staff of LTV Corporation as a lobbyist and had a lot of Washington "street smarts." The NCPC staff personnel were cordial, courteous and bemused by the intrepid duo who were charging into the bureaucracy of monument building in Washington; the two looked like emissaries they had entertained from several other "well intended" groups. It was a part of their job. While they were open in their response and outlined the negative aspects of attempting to undertake such a project, they offered some suggestions as to available sites. Franklin Park, a large city block at the southwest sector of the intersection of K and 14th Streets, would be a "nice place for the bands to play." Also, two sites remained on Pennsylvania Avenue, which was being redeveloped by the Pennsylvania avenue Development Corporation (PADC).

With no hesitation, Brett and Thompson called on the PADC to meet with its Vice President in charge of Development, Charles Gueli. Gueli recited the "corporation's desire to bring life back to the avenue..." and evinced some intrigue and interest in an amphitheater in the middle of the redevelopment parcel. The PADC was a federally chartered, quasi-government corporation charged with the responsibility to redevelop Pennsylvania Avenue between the Capitol and the White House.

The story goes that at the end of his Inaugural Parade down the "Avenue of the Presidents," President Kennedy told his aide Patrick Moynihan that something had to be done about the shabby condition of Pennsylvania Avenue. It was a disgrace to the nation that "Main Street, USA," the boulevard connecting the executive mansion with the legislative domicile, the nation's Capitol, should be in such deplorable condition. Subsequent legislative action produced the PADC which was funded by the Congress but it could buy and sell real estate on the avenue in the redevelopment process, keeping costs to a minimum.

As redevelopment of Pennsylvania Avenue progressed, the project gained recognition as an historic urban renewal program, a classic case demonstrating what could be accomplished when government and business sectors cooperated in a common effort. With Pershing Square and the majestic Willard Hotel on the Western end to the Canadian Chancellery which anchors the Eastern terminus, today The Avenue is transforming into a stately, prestigious, functional thoroughfare which is befitting of its national prominence.

Single Up All Lines!

Although the PADC staff wasn't overly enthusiastic about having the "Navy," as the Foundation was labeled, occupy a prize site on Pennsylvania Avenue, the concept grew in favor because its basic feature, an amphitheater, would help restore life to the Avenue. An element of anti-militarism prevailed, but was based on fear that a monstrous organization, the "Navy," was trying to take over sacred land.

Generally, patriotism and appreciation for the military was on the rise in the early 1980's. An argument heard was that "...outdoor concerts are fine but what happens there during the other nine months of the year?" Andrew Barnes, PADC Executive Director, wondered if an ice rink could be installed for the winter months, but this melted away when it was realized that two ice rinks already existed in the area. Other common arguments were, "Why should the Navy have a prime

site? What if the other services want a memorial? Why not a memorial to the Armed Forces?"

Thompson and other members of the board of directors countered that the Marine Corps already had its national memorial in the Iwo Jima Monument; the Army had the Tomb of the Unknown in the Arlington National Cemetery; the Air Force has concentrated on its museum at Wright-Patterson Air Force Base in Dayton, Ohio and was very strong in the Smithsonian Air and Space Museum and the Coast Guard claimed a national memorial in Arlington Cemetery. As for an Armed Forces Memorial, Foundation members dismissed it as unfundable unless the government would underwrite it. Individual service alumni would contribute to "their"

memorial but not to an all encompassing Armed Forces Memorial.

Rationale as to why there should be a Navy Memorial was that although there were many Navy related memorials in Washington, such as Farragut Square, DuPont Circle and one of the most beautiful sculptures in Washington—the wave action with seven sea gulls in flight, in Lady Bird Park on Virginia's George Washington Parkway—none was dedicated to the Navy, only to individuals or units of the Navy.

Additionally, Navy has always had its headquarters in Washington while the Army and Air Force have scattered theirs throughout the country. Washington was definitely Navy's homeport with the Naval Academy close by and the Washington Navy Yard so rich in history that paralleled that of the city and nation.

Thomas Regan was the director of operations for the PADC when the dialogue between the Foundation and PADC began. He was at all times circumspect and non-parochial regarding the Navy Memorial proposal, even though he was a member of the graduating class of 1965 at the Naval Academy and was a civil engineer while on active duty. He definitely endorsed it and was instrumental in having the proposal adopted by the PADC board. He counseled Thompson in maneuvering the proposal around Washington and before the PADC board, but always in the context, "If you really want to do this and want this site, this is my recommendation. Take it for what it's worth."

Thompson considered Regan's recommendations to be "top dollar" and he appreciated his relationship with Tom Regan, bound initially by the simple threads of Navy Blue and Gold and maturing to one of mutual respect and trust. Even when Regan moved up to the top paid position, Executive Director, in the staff, the relationship continued. When he left the PADC, Thompson nominated him as a director of the Foundation and made him Vice President, Construction.

PADC's board of directors approved the concept for the Navy Memorial to be built in Market Square, a two-and-a-half acre parcel of land on the north side of Pennsylvania Avenue between Seventh and Ninth Streets, across from the National Archives. It had been a market place at one time, hence its name.

Archives Station, on Washington's modern subway system, provides access to rapid mass transportation at the site. Stipulations included that the PADC would approve the design and financing of the project and would serve as contracting agency for construction. So in this process, the Foundation picked up another governing agency to add to the three prescribed by law.

In partnership with the PADC, the Foundation participated in selecting an architect as the first step toward developing a design concept for the Navy Memorial. The Foundation was allowed two seats on a PADC selection committee which ultimately chose Conklin Rossant architectural firm of New York City to be the architect for the memorial and development of Market Square.

With William Conklin, a World War II naval officer, at the helm and Tom Regan, executive director of the PADC staff, at the conn, a design concept was developed which could have added a possible new dimension to naval history. Conklin recommended that the Navy be memorialized in its nation's capital by a massive arch, an Arc de Triomphe lifted almost in entirety from Paris.

With great enthusiasm, the Navy Memorial Foundation board approved the arch concept and pressed hard for its approval. Typical of Navy thinking, it was full speed ahead. A decision had been made, ". . .so get on with it, Mates, and no sky larking along the way."

The arch concept was favorably endorsed by the Commission of Fine Arts, the PADC and the National Park Service. The fourth and final approval was to come from the National Capital Planning Commission, but the momentum came to an abrupt stop and a "fallen arch" resulted from a 9-3 vote against the design concept for reasons that the arch was overpowering to surrounding buildings, threatening to the National Archives across the street and impairing to the sacred vista.

In retrospect, and according to Thompson, the loss of the arch was a blessing because even though Conklin had estimated the cost of the building to be $10 million, it would have escalated to nearly $15,000,000. And fund raising was not easy, especially for the Foundation staff and boardmembers who had spent many years in the sheltered cocoon provided by the military. It was repugnant for many of them to ask for money, even though there was confidence in the cause. Up to that time, fund raising had been difficult because few individuals or corporations wanted to support a project that was nothing more than an idea and now that idea had dissipated.

Three hundred thousand hard gotten dollars had been invested in the arch concept and the Foundation's financial condition was as low as its morale. Many supporters and potential contributors wrote off the U.S. Navy Memorial as "another ship that passed in the night."

However, instead of folding, the Foundation staff returned to "the drawing boards" to redesign a concept. Up to this time, the "staff" comprised Thompson and his ever loyal secretary, Mrs. Donohue, and for the previous year, retired Captain Walt Thomas who worked from 10:00 to 3:00 to avoid traffic, and one or two part time secretarial helpers. Another retired Captain, John Davey, worked briefly as a direct mail consultant. Tom Regan, Conklin Rossant and Thompson worked diligently to formulate ideas but nothing evolved except more frustration for the Foundation. Even the PADC was becoming uneasy because it wanted to start

construction at Market Square, the last undeveloped parcel in their domain.

Thompson, now the Foundation President, did something unusual in the Washington bureaucracy. He formed an Ad Hoc committee comprising executive directors of all the approving agencies plus others in the District of Columbia government to oversee the development of a new concept. Its purpose was to thrash out all possible caveats and gain unofficial approval of a concept before attempting the official approval process.

With the help of Captain Thomas, Stanley Bleifeld, the Foundation's designated sculptor, and John Roach, a marine artist and Naval Reservist, a basic design was created which developed and matured to completion and is the Navy Memorial as it exists today. It was then turned over to Conklin Rossant, who had worked with the Foundation group, for refinement and architectural-engineering work. With the informal endorsement of the Ad Hoc committee, the design was finally approved by all agencies in June 1984.

The new Navy Memorial design was an abrupt change from the massive, dominating arch concept. As it is now, a relatively low profile is presented by the amphitheater which is a 100-foot circle surrounded by four large pools, each with moving water. The two large pools abutting Pennsylvania Avenue have several water jets which provide needed verticality.

Tom Regan made the statement after he had left the PADC to become a real estate developer in the Washington Area, that ". . .within five years, Market Square will be the Rockefeller Center of Washington and its center piece will be the Navy Memorial."

"Cast Off All Lines"

Next, the Navy Memorial Foundation set about to select a sculptor, who working with the architect, would help design various aesthetic elements of the Navy Memorial, including the statuary. A selection board procedure, similar to that employed by the Navy, was initiated and PADC architectural consultant Sasaki Associates assisted in culling the nation's files for eligible candidates. Every conceivable sculptor was investigated

initially by Sasaki and 36 were looked at by a board of eight people representing the art world and the Foundation's board of directors. Five finalists were chosen and each of those were checked out, including interviews and visits to their studios.

Another group of panelists reviewed elaborately prepared dossiers and portfolios and finally selected Stanley Bleifeld of Weston, Connecticut, ending a seven month search for a Navy Memorial artist.

After ensuing congratulations and early conversations, it was found that Bleifeld had been in the Navy as an enlisted man during world War II, a fact that was not revealed in his biographical data. However, it didn't make much difference in Bleifeld's nautical background except that he had worn the uniform and had some vague familiarity with it. He was from Brooklyn and joined the Navy to "see the world" and got as far as Bainbridge, Maryland for "boot camp" before returning to New York City to spend the rest of the war illustrating training manuals. He lived at home much of that time.

Bleifeld arrived on the Navy Memorial scene at the time the Memorial Arch was in its last months. His job was to work with the architect to design the adornments that would make the arch "sing" as well as look nautical. His immediate reaction to the arch was negative and that attitude did not change, although his demeanor was circumspect and gentlemanly. After the arch fell, he began to illustrate his thoughts for a Navy memorial. One sketch he presented informally to the staff contained various naval features and overlooking the entire seascape was a lone figure, a sailor, huddled in a peacoat, braving inclement conditions. The lone figure was obviously only an adornment to the main thrust of the presentation but both Admiral Thompson and Captain Thomas agreed that no matter what happened to the rest of the work, "the lone sailor stays." That was the beginning of the "Lone Sailor" statue that was going to bring Bleifeld fame and fortune.

Bleifeld worked on the basic memorial concept and made valuable contributions. Simultaneously, he was pushed to develop the Lone Sailor which was then perceived to be the central piece of statuary in the memorial. Five generations of the Lone Sailor were produced, four in clay model form and the fifth in a painting.

In mid stream, Thompson and Thomas prepared a narrative description of the Lone Sailor and psyche of its characterization. The final versions were figures to which anyone who had ever been to sea, Navy or otherwise, could relate. The third version was the Lone Sailor, but in a more informal pose, one foot on a mooring cleat, elbow resting on his knee, gazing out to sea. Everyone in the staff literally "fell in love" with this model. He was a sailor! A fun loving sailor! Ready to take on the world. But he wasn't as serious and seaworthy as was desired in the Lone Sailor characterization.

His successor is just that, developed first in a painting and finally in a clay model. He is the Lone Sailor, the only piece of statuary to be placed in the amphitheater and undoubtedly will be the enduring art form of the Navy Memorial.

The Lone Sailor's predecessor was dubbed "Liberty Hound" and has attained popularity and his own charisma. A full scale bronze of the "Liberty Hound" will be the center piece of a Navy Memorial in Jacksonville, Florida and will take on a more dignified status, including losing his frivolous nickname.

Navy veteran Stanley Bleifeld at work in his Connecticut studio. The Lone Sailor required more than a year to perfect.

An early model of the Lone Sailor was criticized for its mirth, light-heartedness and casual stance.

Although the Lone Sailor was approved by all concerned, there was a miniscule element of disfavor, possibly because his characterization was not understood. Hands in his pockets and peacoat unbuttoned were the negative comments voiced by the few dissenters. Thompson's reply was that "...this is a piece of art, a representation of a young second class petty officer who is alone, physically and in his own thoughts, as he contemplates the vast oceans which, in the seven or so years he has been in the Navy, he has come to respect, admire and fear their changing moods as well as their romantic beauty.

As the saying goes, 'There is some wind in his canvas' as he braves the elements. His hands are in his pockets because they are cold. That's why the Navy put pockets in peacoats. His collar is up because of the same inclement conditions. This statue is much more profound, more symbolically significant and more human than would be characterized by a figure standing at attention, ready for inspection. This one figure symbolizes all who have served in the Navy since 1775. That hasn't been easy to come by, but the reaction to the Lone Sailor thus far has been overwhelmingly favorable by those who have served in the Navy and others, including those from the art world and those who romanticize about the Navy. They relate to the Lone Sailor and like him.

Plans for additional statuary, depending on availability of funds, include a woman as well as a black sailor, which would be smaller than the Lone Sailor and placed in the front pools. A coalition of Navy women's groups has sponsored a bas-relief which will depict their history in the Navy and has also pledged to sponsor a female statue.

The Navy Memorial honors people and their accomplishments, successes and sacrifices. One aspect of Navy life that will be drawn into the artistic elements is the Navy family and the contributions made by those who are normally left at home.

The Fleet Reserve Association, made up of enlisted personnel of the "sea services," but with the Navy far outnumbering the Marine Corps and Coast Guard,

Home from the Sea

ARTIST RENDERING of the Homecoming statue by sculptor Stanley Bleifeld which will be placed north of the bandstand at the United States Navy Memorial. This life-size grouping depicts dockside scenes of sailors and loved ones reunited upon the return to port of Navy ships following deployment. Sponsorship of the Homecoming is by the Fleet Reserve Association (FRA) as part of their $1 million pledge to the Navy Memorial.

pledged $1,000,000 to the Memorial, concentrating on the "Homecoming" statue. This piece of art work, being done by Bleifeld, first appeared in one of his initial renderings. It characterizes a young sailor, returning from an extended cruise, being welcomed home by his wife and child on the pier, a scene familiar to all who have been in, or a part of, the Navy.

There will be 22 bas-reliefs on the southern periphery of the amphitheater, each one a 30x36-inch bronze depicting an important event in Navy history or recognizing a group or unit which contributed to the success of the Navy and the development of the country. Most of these art pieces will be sponsored by organizations, corporations or ad hoc groups interested in the project or a specific naval subject. The FRA Auxiliary has volunteered to sponsor a bas-relief about the Navy family. The first bas-relief to be cast is the "Women in the Navy"; another sponsored by the

Destroyer Escort Sailors Association will show the advent of the destroyer escorts in World War II and the Construction Battalions, the "Seabees," will be sponsored by their association. More than 35 potential subjects are being considered by the Foundation.

The two flag poles which guard the ceremonial area at the entrance to the amphitheater will be ringed by bas-relief continuums, chronicling the development of the Navy through a graphic description of ships, submarines and aircraft. The ceremonial space itself is a large bronze casting of a compass rose, encircled by bronze rings and white granite. This is where the Foundation envisions wreath laying ceremonies on significant holidays or by visiting dignitaries.

Before setting the last stone in place, Admiral Thompson "buries" a computer tape listing all of the names already entered in the Navy Memorial Log.

The large southwest pool takes on an international aspect, it being dedicated to navies that have sailed with, fought alongside and gone to sea in common causes, with the U.S. Navy. Countries that have helped to sponsor the Memorial by contributing to its construction, will have their names inscribed on the wall. Argentina was the first country to contribute to the U.S. Navy Memorial, followed by Spain, France, the Republic of China (Taiwan), Japan, the Republic of Korea and Australia. Argentina made its contribution shortly after the Falkland Islands' conflict which led to a request of the British government which has been unanswered for more than three years. When asked to comment, Thompson shrugged and said: "It would be a bloody shame to not have the British Navy represented in our memorial because of the close association our navies have had over the years. Many of our traditions have been derived from the British Navy. We want them to be a part of our memorial."

The deck of the amphitheater posed some problems, first in the design and second in production. Although Conklin Rossant continually presented squared-off or rectangular amphitheater designs, Thompson's team preferred a circle. It wasn't until he attended a meeting in downtown Washington that he saw a polar projection of the world on the bottom of an ashtray. Borrowing the ashtray, he made a hurried return to his office to announce the discovery of the amphitheater's deck. From then on it was working with the Defense Mapping Agency and Conklin Rossant until an acceptable polar projection could be attained. What resulted was one that centers on Washington, D.C. and shows about 90 percent of the world's land mass and the vastness of the ocean areas, the Navy's domain. This two-color granite map is the largest in the world. A special Laurentide Blue granite from the Laurentian Mountains in Canada represent the oceans and a Deer Isle Gray, from Deer Island in Maine, for land. And the granite is two inches thick, giving the map the undisputed heavyweight title, weighing in at 217,634 pounds.

Cutting the map presented a problem to the stone cutting contractors, New England Stone Corporation of Smithfield, Rhode Island. An advanced technology machine was to be devised to cut what was essentially a jigsaw puzzle, except that two cuts were necessary, one to shape the beaches and the other the Laurentide blue water. A machine which was already in existence to cut metals and even bakery goods, was modified to cut granite. With a few modifications, a new machine was born and introduced to the stone cutting industry, one which will have a lasting effect for stone cutters everywhere. It is a computer guided water jet cutting tool, developing up to 60,000 psi, that will cut almost anything and has significantly reduced the time and cost of cutting stone.

A Following Sea

The second phase of the Memorial is the Visitors Center which will be housed in a mixed-use, office, residential and retail building on the northeast perimeter of the amphitheater. it will feature a 250 seat theater, to be used primarily for motion picture presentations and, at other times, for seminars on nautical subjects. Function rooms, offices and a "Ship's Store" will occupy the remaining space, except for the Navy Memorial Log Room. The Log Room will exist to support a basic fund raising program adopted by the Foundation. Similar to other popular contributor presentation programs, it has developed an appeal of its own that has been enthusiastically supported by Navy veterans.

The log comprises names of Navy veterans on whose behalf a minimum of $25 has been contributed to the memorial construction fund. In the Log Room, all names will be scrolled continuously and a second presentation provides for a name to be "called up" from a keyboard to have the veteran's full name, highest rate or rank attained, period of service and date and place of birth. This will be presented on a large screen or "score board" display. It has proved popular for individuals to enter their own names, a gift for Father's or Mother's Day or Christmas, or to sponsor relatives or shipmates. Special groups such as those killed in the USS Liberty on June 8, 1967 have been sponsored by individuals and benevolent organizations. The 37 men killed in the USS Stark in the Persian Gulf on May 17, 1987 were sponsored by several organizations. Also, shipmates from yesteryears have been memorialized in the log such as the entire crew of Captain John Paul Jones' Continental Navy Ship Bonhomme Richard. Manifests of these ships are available from the Navy Department or the National Archives. At the time of Dedication,

some 95,000 names had been entered in the Navy Memorial Log.

Raising the funds necessary to support such an ambitious project, has not been easy. The staff and directors of the Foundation were, by and large, Navy careerists, who found it to be anathematic to ask others for money. Admiral Thomas Moorer, a supporter of many Navy related projects, said,

"It only becomes honorable when it is evident that it is absolutely necessary if the project is to survive."

Fund raising professionals and experts aver that 10% of the donors will give 90 percent of the money and encourage efforts be directed toward potential big contributors. The Navy Memorial has been supported by large contributions such as Grumman Corporation at more than $250,000, General Dynamics at $225,000 and the Fleet Reserve Association at $1,000,000, but it has benefited from a much broader base of support. About half of its monies have come from individuals, usually Navy veterans, who contribute $25 or more to enter the Navy Log. In acknowledging that statistic, Board Chairman John G. Tower, said, "It is an arduous way to raise funds but it is heartwarming to have that broad acceptance of our project. It also buoys the confidence of the board of directors and the staff. It is also another signal that the Navy family is a large, but close-knit group."

What has been wrought in Market Square on Pennsylvania Avenue is a "living" Memorial that is functional in its many aspects. It is a place where visitors can be entertained, can relax in the plaza, be educated about some of the Nation's heritage, particularly about its Navy, or be thrilled by an exciting movie about the fun, zest and adventure of the seas, the Navy's habitat. It also has the sanctity of a memorial that honors those who have served and some who have perished helping to provide peace and security to this maritime Nation.

Retired Captain Robert T. Jones, Thompson's deputy for the past three years is confident that the Memorial complex will take its place alongside other major memorials in Washington and will be on the "must see lists" for tourists and tours. While it honors all who have served in the Navy, it is also a tribute to the Foundation's Board of Directors, its staff, its sponsors and all who helped in its construction.

On Dedication Day, a Navy signal was appropriately hoisted at the Memorial: A "BRAVO ZULU (Well Done) to All Hands."

© *Stanley Bleifeld*

The Lone Sailor:

Mr. Bleifeld's initial rendering of the Lone Sailor was one-quarter the size of the finished statue. Five different Washington agencies approved the rendering before Mr. Bleifeld could scale up to a full-sized clay model. When the clay version was approved, Mr. Bleifeld packed the model with a plaster coating to make a negative mold, and, the last step in his Connecticut studios, created a plaster positive to ship to the Tallix Foundry in Beacon, New York.

The Tallix Foundry, specializing in service to the art community, is owned by Richard Polich, who was a commissioned naval officer in the late 1950s. Mr. Polich completed the jet aircraft training syllabus in November, 1957, and flew the Navy's F-9 jet fighters until he left active duty in 1959 as a Lieutenant Junior Grade.

Tallix used Bleifeld's positive to pour sectional rubber negatives, and these were used to make positive wax molds 3/16ths of an inch thick, the thickness of the hollow bronze shell unveiled today. Tallix craftsmen carefully cleaned the wax positives and attached to them an elaborate system of wax runners or gates. Then they surrounded the wax tubes and shells, inside and out, with a strong ceramic shell.

Each ceramic shell was autoclaved to a temperature of 1800-degrees Fahrenheit, the wax positive was lost— melted out of the remaining mold— leaving space for the final pouring of bronze, which occurred on August 4, 1987.

At the request of Mr. Bleifeld and Rear Admiral William Thompson, USN (Ret.), President of the Navy Memorial Foundation, Mr. Polich had his workers melt into the bronze for the Lone Sailor, artifacts from eight U.S. Navy ships, provided by Henry A. Vadnais, Jr., Curator for the Navy in the Naval Historical Center at the Washington Navy Yard.

The ships span the Navy's history, yielding small pieces of copper sheeting, spikes, hammock hooks, a section of a brass voice tube, a copper bolt and a section of railing. There is a piece of *USS Ranger* commissioned in 1876, as the country celebrated its Centennial. She

THE LONE SAILOR statue is a composite of the U.S. Navy bluejacket, past, present and future.

He is 25 years old at most, a senior second class petty officer who is fast becoming a seagoing veteran. He has done it all—fired his weapons in a dozen wars, weighed anchor from a thousand ports, tracked supplies, doused fires, repelled boarders, typed in quadruplicate and mess-cooked, too. He has made liberty call in great cities and tiny villages, where he played tourist, ambassador, missionary to the poor, adventurer, souvenir shopper and friend to new lands. His shipmates remember him with pride and tell their grandchildren stories, some of which, like him, are seven feet tall.

The Lone Sailor is the creation of Stanley Bleifeld, the U.S. Navy Memorial's official sculptor. Mr. Bleifeld served in the Navy in World War II, and like many other talented artists at the time, he was assigned as an illustrator for Navy training manuals. He never went into battle, but he helped train those who did.

Creative Concept to Casting

was an iron-hulled steamer, but still depended on her full sail rig when cruising on distant station. *USS Constitution* and *USS Constellation* are here, representing the early years of the United States when our independence was tested and reconfirmed in the Quasi-War with France, the Barbary Wars and the War of 1812. These two ships still exist, the *Constellation* as the centerpiece of Baltimore's Inner Harbor and *Constitution* in Boston Harbor. The steamer *Hartford* is here, flagship of Admiral David G. Farragut, in the Civil War era. There is also a fragment from *USS Maine*, a battleship commissioned in 1895, whose destruction in Havana Harbor on February 15, 1895 touched off our War with Spain.

The Navy's hard fighting cruisers of World War II are represented by a part of *USS Biloxi*, symbolic of the ships which formed the backbone of the Navy's striking force in the bloody battles of the Solomon Islands. Also represented is *USS Hancock*, a reminder of the illustrious record of our aircraft carriers (flattops) in World War II. Finally, there is a fragment from *USS Seawolf*, the world's second nuclear-propelled vehicle, built at the same time as *USS Nautilus*. These bits of metal are now part of the Lone Sailor.

After the bronze sections were poured, cooled and sandblasted, the foundry welded them together for the very last step, patination—a heat and chemical treatment to achieve controlled oxidation yielding the distinctive color of the statue as it appears today.

Mr. Bleifeld worked on the Lone Sailor creation for more than a year, and the technical processes took several additional months, with all of the effort focused on unveiling at the dedication.

In addition to the Lone Sailor, the Navy Memorial will house other sculptures of Stanley Bleifeld, including "Homecoming," depicting a pierside reunion of a Navy man and his wife and son. Another statue will honor foreign navies. ⊤

"Let us always remember the sacrifices of those who have given their lives in peacetime and in conflict."

"Sailors are among the hardest working people in uniform today."

It is most fitting that we dedicate the United States Navy Memorial during this, the year we celebrate the bicentennial of our Constitution. While the United States Navy was born during our Revolutionary War, it is the opening paragraph of our Constitution, ratified by our new nation 12 years later, that serves as its foundation: "in order to...provide for the common defense...secure the blessings of freedom to ourselves and our posterity..."

For these 200 years our Constitution has been the model for governance by the rule of law established by the will of the people. And during these 200 years, the men and women who have served in the Navy have indeed "secured the blessings of freedom."

This memorial commemorates in steel and concrete the gratitude of a nation that has been well served throughout its history by its Navy. Let us always remember the sacrifices of those who have given their lives in peacetime and in conflict. And let us also always remember the dedication of all who have served in the Navy. This is the true spirit of the Navy Memorial.

The Honorable Caspar W. Weinberger
Secretary of Defense

America is a maritime nation. Our strategic interests have been relatively constant over the decades, dictated by our insular position and the location of our international commitments. As the Navy Memorial's circular plaza bearing an inlaid, granite map of the world will clearly show, we have no choice but to maintain naval superiority as the keystone of our global strategy.

The Navy Memorial is a symbol for all of us, a symbol for America, of the sacrifices Navy people and their families have made throughout our Nation's history to keep our country safe and free. It is fitting that this memorial honors the people of the Navy, not technology or hardware; for in the aggregate, sailors are among the hardest working people in uniform today. They are constantly operational and away from their families for extended periods every year. These sacrifices will become tangible to everyone who visits the Navy Memorial.

Reflecting upon the memorial's Lone Sailor causes one to contemplate what a marvelous creature a seagoing sailor is. He can be profane or polite, unapologetic or tactful. He is predictably a tough, uncomplaining worker who knows how to enjoy his liberty. His sacrifices throughout our history have purchased the right to this memorial many times over.

Technologies will change, but the indomitable spirit of the American sailor and his love of freedom will not. May all those who visit the United States Navy Memorial offer a silent prayer of thanks that our country is blessed with the dedicated service of the men and women of the United States Navy.

The Honorable James H. Webb Jr.
Secretary of the Navy

*"In this figure of the Lone
Sailor, rests the spirit of
those who have known the
challenge of the seas."*

*"American sailors have
labored, served, fought and died
so that others might have a
better life in freedom and peace."*

THIS MEMORIAL REPRESENTS a tremendous amount of hard work by a lot of dedicated individuals—both Navy people and friends of Navy people. They have overcome a multitude of problems which inevitably are a part of such a project. The uniqueness of design and advanced construction techniques are testimony to the creativeness of approach and the positive attitude of the people who were charged with the responsibility of bringing this edifice into being.

There is more to this structure, however, than originality of concept and building technology. It is what it represents—honoring all those who have gone down to the sea in ships. In this figure of the Lone Sailor, rests the spirits of those who have known the challenge of the seas. Some have survived the challenge while others have fallen to a ferocity that was beyond human endurance. One characteristic they shared in common was the willingness to meet that challenge in support of one another.

This memorial will stand as a tribute to the dignity of all the "Lone Sailors" who have gone before and who are to follow, their ability to confront the unknown with a stout heart and a keen mind and above all—to serve their country, their service and their shipmates.

The respect we pay to these men and women today has been earned—and will continue to be earned—through sacrifice, bravery, self denial and devotion to duty.

This site will become more than a place for ceremonial events. It will be a lasting and historical location to remember those with whom we share a common heritage—the sea.

Arleigh Burke
Admiral, U.S. Navy (Ret.)
Former Chief of Naval Operations

NAVY MEN AND WOMEN have a great deal to be proud of, and our country should share this pride. For two centuries American sailors have labored, served, fought and died so that others might have a better life in freedom and peace. In the process they have created the world's most respected Navy.

This memorial, coming literally from the heart of America, will serve to remind future generations of the Navy's magnificent history and traditions forged in both peace and war—traditions of achievement, of gallantry, of service, of sacrifice, of victory. My father helped set those high standards as a sailor in World War I. His example, and that of others remembered here, will prod future generations to excel and further tighten the bond between the Navy and our citizenry.

As I have looked over the memorial's design, my eye has been drawn unfailingly to the figure of the Lone Sailor. In more than forty years of service I have acquired a host of memories of grand events, ships, duty stations, and exotic sights. But the dominant image in my mind is that of shipmates and friends sharing the joys, rigors and perils of service life. To me the Lone Sailor statue represents all of my Navy comrades.

Like the people this solitary figure stands for, he will keep his distant watch forever. Like the Navy he represents, he cannot come home from that vigil, or America's children and those in other hopeful societies around the globe will one day pay an enormous price.

Many like him are on duty now on the oceans carrying forward a proud tradition. We are fortunate the Navy attracts such people; those men and women make the Navy worthwhile as a career and way of life, and the world is better and safer because of them.

William J. Crowe, Jr.
Admiral, U.S. Navy
Chairman, Joint Chiefs of Staff

600 Ships. . . and More

John F. Lehman, Jr.
Former Secretary of the Navy

Geographically, alliances, and the Soviet threat combine to dictate the actual numbers of ships—the "size of the Navy"—required to fulfill our commitments in each of our maritime theaters. And this accounting adds up to a 600-ship Navy.

CLEMENCEAU ONCE DECLARED that war was too important to be left to the generals. But if war is too important to be left to the generals, it is also too important to be left to the civilian experts. In the United States, with our constitutionally mandated civilian control of the armed forces, we forget sometimes that hard-earned military experience must leaven the theories of civilians if our system is to work.

We would do well to keep this in mind as we near our goal of a 600-ship Navy. Media-anointed experts have raised questions about the size, character, and complexity of the Navy: Do we really need so many ships? Are the Navy and Marine Corps effective in helping to deter Soviet aggression—across the full spectrum of violence, from terrorism to nuclear war? Do we have a strategy that guides the planning and training of our forces? Is it the correct strategy? If it is, are we building the right types and numbers of ships to execute it? Finally, can this nation afford to sustain a 600-ship fleet—not only well equipped but properly manned—for the long term? When defense restrictions become law in the zero-growth 1986 budget, and retrenchment is the theme of the hour, the answers to these questions take on added significance.

To understand how we arrived at the size of our planned fleet of ships, we must begin by discarding the idea that this number has sprung, full blown, from the brow of some would-be Napoleon of the high seas.

Since World War II, maritime force planners have found themselves at the mercy of three enduring elements. First is geography. Water covers three quarters of the world; and the United States is an "island continent" washed by the Atlantic and Pacific oceans.

Second are the vital interests of the United States, expressed in the web of more than 40 treaty relationships that bind us to mutual defense coalitions around the world. These relationships shape our national security requirements— together with the energy and commercial dependences that support our economy in peace and in war.

The third element is the Soviet threat. Whatever its original rationale, the Soviet Navy's postwar expansion has created an offense-oriented blue water force, a major element in the Soviet Union's global military reach that supports expanding Soviet influence from Nicaragua to Vietnam to Ethiopia. From the Baltic to the Caribbean to the South China Sea, our ships and men pass within yards of Soviet naval forces every day. But familiarity, in this case, is breeding a well-deserved respect.

The Navy's recently updated *Understanding Soviet Naval Developments* provides the facts about the Soviet Navy. Every American should be aware, for example,

JOHN F. LEHMAN, JR., left office in April 1987 after serving six years as one of the youngest men ever to hold the position of Secretary of the Navy. A Commander in the Naval Reserve, Lehman flies A-6 aircraft and is assigned to Medium Attack Wing One, Naval Air Station, Oceana, Virginia.

that Soviet nuclear submarines operate continuously off our coasts. "Victor"-class nuclear attack submarines are routinely found lurking near many of our principal naval ports. Soviet surface units are now making regular deployments to the contentious and vulnerable chokepoints of the Caribbean Sea and Gulf of Mexico. Worldwide, we find the Soviet Navy astride the vital sea-lanes and navigational chokepoints, through which most of the Western world's international trade must pass.

This is the new reality. The pattern of Soviet naval deployments has revealed itself in only the last several years. These deployments constitute a post-World War II change in the global military balance of power that has been surpassed only by the advent of thermonuclear weapons. No planner, civilian or military, can ignore the growing dimensions of Soviet maritime power.

Geography, alliances, and the Soviet threat combine to dictate the actual numbers of ships—the "size of the Navy"—required to fulfill our commitments in each of our maritime theaters. Before reviewing in detail the forces we need in each theater, some observations are in order:

- Any view of the global disposition of the U.S. Navy reveals that we often deploy in peacetime very much in the same manner as we would operate in wartime. For purposes of deterrence, crisis management, and diplomacy, we must be present in the areas where we would have to fight if war broke out. Of course, the operational tempo is different—a roughly three-to-one ratio in wartime, as compared with peacetime.

We also train as we intend to fight. A full-scale general war at sea would rarely find a carrier battle group operating alone. So we train often in multiple carrier battle forces in such exercises as FLEETEX, READEX, and NATO exercises, like Northern Wedding, which we conduct in the North Atlantic and the Norwegian Sea.

- Our maritime security depends on significant

Line handlers (left) aboard *USS Thorn* stand ready for underway refueling in heavy seas from the fleet oiler *USS Merrimack.*

assistance from allies in executing our missions. Fortunately, we count among our friends all of the world's great navies, save one. Clearly, in areas such as diesel submarines, frigates, coastal patrol craft, minesweepers, and maritime patrol aircraft, allies of the United States have assets absolutely essential to us for sea control in war and peace. In some regions, such as the Eastern Atlantic and the waters surrounding the United Kingdom, our allies supply a significant portion of the antisubmarine capability to counter the Soviet threat. In fact, if we could not count on our allies, we would require a U.S. fleet much larger than 600 ships to deal with the 1,700 ships and submarines that the Soviets can deploy against us. But the world's greatest navies are on our side, and this gives a tremendous advantage to the U.S. Navy and a significant cost savings to the U.S. taxpayer.

■ America's increasing commercial and energy interdependence with Asia, and the growth of the Soviet Pacific Fleet—now the largest of the four Soviet fleets—have negated the so-called "swing strategy" of the Sixties and Seventies, which planned to reinforce the Atlantic Fleet with combatants from the Pacific in time of crisis. Today, the United States has an Asian orientation at least equal to its historic engagement in Europe. Existing treaty relationships in the Pacific have been augmented by growing commercial connections. For example, in 1980, the value of U.S. trade with the Pacific rim nations was roughly equal to trade with the country's Atlantic partners. Four years later, Pacific trade exceeded that with Western Europe by $26 billion.

Similarly, oil dependencies have shifted tremendously in the last five years. This forces America to reconsider the priorities of naval deployments in the Northern

Pacific and Caribbean regions. The re-orientation of U.S. sources for crude oil—on a hemispheric axis—is a long-term geopolitical reality that has gone largely unnoticed. Western dependency on Middle Eastern oil is still debated at length, for its impact on our military thinking and force planning. But we must also take into account that, in 1985, the United States imported eight times as much oil by sea from the Western Hemisphere as it received from the entire Middle East. Oil from Mexico has increased to almost 25% of our imports, while oil from Saudi Arabia has dropped to only 2.6% of the U.S. import market. We no longer depend primarily on the Middle East and Persian Gulf supply for our vital energy needs. Instead, the locus of our oil trade is in the Western Hemisphere: Alaska, Canada, Mexico, Venezuela, and the Caribbean area.

With these observations as background, let us review our forces in the main geographic areas: the Atlantic, the Mediterranean, the Pacific, and Indian Ocean-Persian Gulf. The numbers used are "notional." They illustrate force packages constructed for peacetime tasks now assigned to our naval forces. But they are capable of expansion or contraction, should war break out—a flexibility characteristic of naval powers.

The Atlantic: The large Atlantic theater encompasses the North Atlantic, the Norwegian Sea, the Northern Flank of NATO including the Baltic throat, the South Atlantic, the Caribbean, and the Gulf of Mexico. It includes the coasts of South America and the west coast of Africa, all vital sea-lanes of communications. And it involves the Mediterranean and the Middle East.

The U.S. Navy operates in the Atlantic theater with two fleets, the Sixth and the Second. The Sixth Fleet in the Mediterranean is the principal fighting force of the NATO Southern Europe Command and provides strike, antiair superiority, antisubmarine, and close air support for the entire Southern Flank of NATO—a principal makeweight in the balance in the Central Front.

In addition, the Sixth Fleet is the principal naval force that supports our friends and allies in the Middle East. The threat there is significant. The Soviets maintain a fleet in the Black Sea and a deployed squadron in the Mediterranean. In wartime, we expect to see also Soviet naval strike aircraft, aircraft carriers, a formidable number of diesel and nuclear submarines, and a full range of strike cruisers, destroyers, and other smaller combatants.

To deal with this threat, as we do in all our planning, we start with a base of allied forces in the areas under consideration. The navies of our allies are good. For example, we count on them to provide about 140 diesel submarines, which are effective for coastal and area defense, for establishing and maintaining barriers, and for certain other useful missions.

In wartime, purely U.S. forces in the Sixth Fleet would have to include three or four carrier battle groups, operating to meet NATO commitments. We would also need to deploy a battleship surface action group and two underway replenishment groups. In peacetime, we average over the year one and one-third carrier battle groups deployed in the Mediterranean.

The Second Fleet is the heart of the Atlantic strike fleet for NATO. It is responsible for naval operations in

At left, an aircraft carrier battle group underway in the Indian Ocean; at right, missile compartment aboard a Los Angeles-class attack submarine.

the North Atlantic, the Eastern Atlantic, Iceland, the Norwegian Sea, the defense of Norway, and the entire Northern Flank including the North Sea and Baltic throat. It must simultaneously accomplish any naval missions required in the Caribbean, where we now face a very large Soviet and Cuban naval presence; in the South Atlantic, where we have vital sea-lanes; and along the West African sea-lanes, where the Soviets now deploy naval forces continuously.

For the Second Fleet, in wartime, we must plan to have four or five carrier battle groups, one battleship surface action group, and three underway replenishment groups. This is the equivalent firepower of 40 World War II carriers and can deliver accurate strike ordnance on target equal to 800 B-17s every day. In peacetime, we generally run higher than this, because most of our principal training occurs in the Second Fleet's operating areas.

Today, we have six carrier battle groups cycling in the Second Fleet at one time or another. We have exercises underway with our NATO allies, with our South American and Central American allies, and with other nations, on an ad hoc basis, in every season of the year.

The Pacific: Clearly, our increasing commercial interests and historic security ties in the Pacific impact on our naval planning for the area. If we are to protect our vital interests, we must have forces available to deploy—not only to the Atlantic theaters and the Sixth and the Second fleets—but also to the Pacific simultaneously, the Seventh and the Third fleets and the Middle East Force of the Central Command. We cannot abandon one theater in order to deal with the other. The great paradox of the 1970s was the reduction of the fleet's size so that it could only be employed in a swing strategy—just as that strategy was being-rendered obsolete by trade, geopolitics, and the growth of the Soviet Navy.

The Seventh Fleet is our forward Western Pacific fleet, which meets our commitments to Japan, Korea, the Philippines, Australia, New Zealand, and Thailand, and in the critical straits of Southeast Asia, as well as the Indian Ocean. In wartime, we would need to deploy five carrier battle groups to the Seventh Fleet, two battleship surface action groups, and four underway replenishment groups. In peacetime, we average over the year the equivalent of one and one-third carrier battle groups in the Western Pacific. That, of course, helps us maintain a peacetime fleetwide operational tempo that provides for at least 50% time in home port for our people and their families.

We do not have a separate fleet in the critical area of Southwest Asia, the Indian Ocean, and the Persian Gulf,

although some have proposed the re-creation of the Fifth Fleet for that purpose. In peacetime, we have the Middle East Force of the Central Command and elements of the Seventh Fleet, normally a carrier battle group.

In wartime, we plan for two of the Seventh Fleet carrier battle groups to meet our commitments in the Indian Ocean, Southwest Asia, East Africa, the Persian Gulf area, and Southeast Asia. Notionally, a Seventh Fleet battleship surface action group and one underway replenishment group would also be assigned to operate in these areas.

The Third Fleet has the responsibility for operations off Alaska, the Bering Sea, the Aleutians, the Eastern Pacific, and the Mid-Pacific region. In wartime, there would be considerable overlapping and trading back and forth between the Seventh and Third fleets. This happened in the Pacific during World War II. To cover that vast area, we must assign two carrier battle groups and one underway replenishment group.

These requirements compel us to deploy a 600-ship Navy as indicated. In peacetime, we deploy in the same way to the same places we must control in war, but at one-third the tempo of operations. This allows a bearable peacetime burden of six-month deployment lengths and 50% time in home ports. Looked at either way, we require the same size fleet to meet peacetime deployments as we do to fight a war. Taken together they add up to the following:

- Fifteen carrier battle groups
- Four battleship surface action groups
- One-hundred attack submarines
- An adequate number of ballistic missile submarines
- Lift for the assault echelons of a Marine amphibious force and a Marine amphibious brigade

When escort, mine warfare, auxiliary, and replenishment units are considered, about 600 ships emerge from this accounting—a force that can be described as prudent, reflecting geographic realities, alliance commitments and dependencies, and the Soviet fleet that threatens them. Unless Congress reduces our commitments or the Soviet threat weakens, there is no way to reduce the required size of the U.S. fleet and still carry out the missions assigned to the Navy.

At left, the battleship *USS Iowa* fires her 16-inch guns; above, Combat Information Center aboard *USS John F. Kennedy*; at right, open missile silos aboard the trident submarine *USS Georgia*.

United States Navy Battle Forces

(Projected as of September 30, 1988)

Active

	Atlantic Fleet	Pacific Fleet	Combined
Strategic Forces			
Submarine			
Nuclear Ballistic Missile			
Submarine	29	8	37
TOTAL TYPE	29	8	37
Mobile Logistic Ship			
Submarine Tender	4	—	4
TOTAL TYPE	4	—	4
TOTAL CATEGORY	33	8	41
Battle Forces			
Aircraft Carrier	5	4	9
Nuclear-Powered Aircraft Carrier	2	3	5
TOTAL TYPE	7	7	14
Surface Combatants			
Battleship	1	2	3
Guided Missile Cruiser	13	16	29
Nuclear-Powered Guided Missile Cruiser	4	5	9
Destroyer	16	15	31
Guided Missile Destroyer	23	14	37
Frigate	25	26	51
Guided Missile Frigate	25	15	40
TOTAL TYPE	107	93	200
Submarine			
Submarine	1	3	4
Nuclear-Powered Submarine	57	39	96
TOTAL TYPE	58	42	100
Patrol Combatants			
Patrol Combatant Missiles (Hydrofoil)	6	—	6
TOTAL TYPE	6	—	6
Amphibious Warfare Ship			
Command and Control Ship	1	1	2
Amphibious Assault Ship	2	3	5
Amphibious Cargo Ship	2	3	5
Amphibious Transport Dock	6	7	13
Amphibious Assault Ship	4	3	7
Dock Landing Ship	6	6	12
Tank Landing Ship	9	9	18
TOTAL TYPE	30	32	62
Combat Logistic Ship			
Amphibious Ship	5	7	12
Combat Store Ship	3	4	7
Oiler	5	2	7
Fast Combat Support Ship	2	2	4
Replenishment Oiler	3	4	7
TOTAL TYPE	18	19	37

	Atlantic Fleet	Pacific Fleet	Combined
Mine Warfare Ship			
Mine Countermeasure	1	1	2
Mine Sweeper, Ocean	3	—	3
TOTAL TYPE	4	1	5
TOTAL CATEGORY	230	194	424
Support Forces			
Mobile Logistic Ship			
Destroyer Tender	5	4	9
Repair Ship	1	1	2
Submarine Tender	5	3	8
TOTAL TYPE	11	8	19
Support Ships			
Miscellaneous Command Ship	1	1	2
Repair Ship, Small	1	—	1
Salvage Ship	5	3	8
Submarine Reserve Ship	4	2	6
Fleet Ocean Tug	2	—	2
Salvage and Rescue Ship	1	2	3
TOTAL TYPE	14	8	22
TOTAL CATEGORY	25	16	41
Total Active Ship Battle Forces	288	218	506

Reserve

	Atlantic Fleet	Pacific Fleet	Combined
Mobilization Forces, Category A			
Surface Combatants			
Destroyer	1	—	1
Frigate	4	4	8
Guided Missile Frigate	8	8	16
TOTAL TYPE	13	12	25
Amphibious Warfare Ship			
Tank Loading Ship	1	1	2
TOTAL TYPE	1	1	2
Mine Warfare Ship			
Mine Countermeasure Ship	1	—	1
TOTAL TYPE	1	—	1
Total Category Mobilization Force A	15	13	28
Military Sealift Command Ships			44

Total Ship Battle Forces 578

The Navy's Role in the National Strategy

While the Carter administration questioned whether the Navy could influence a "short war" in Central Europe, such a proposition is indefensible today. The coalition of free nations bound together in NATO must have maritime superiority as a prerequisite for any defense strategy. Maritime superiority alone may not assure victory but the loss of it will certainly assure defeat—and sooner rather than later. The chronicles of warfare from the classical era forward are a consistent testament to the influence of sea power upon history, in which great continental powers do not long prevail against an opponent with mastery of the seas. Today, continental defense in NATO rests on early achievement of maritime superiority. The Soviet Union, as evidenced by its ongoing naval expansion, understands the experience of history far better than our trendier military reformists.

Now, consider the charge leveled by some parlor room Pershings that our current naval buildup lacks an underlying strategy.

Not since the days of Theodore Roosevelt have the Navy and Marine Corps exhibited such a strong consensus on the comprehensive strategy which now forms our naval planning. Briefly stated, our strategic objectives are the following:

- To prevent the seas from becoming a hostile medium of attack against the United States and its allies
- To ensure that we have unimpeded use of our ocean lifelines to our allies, our forward-deployed forces, our energy and mineral resources, and our trading partners
- To be able to project force in support of national security objectives and to support combat ashore, should deterrence fail.

To achieve these objectives, we need a strategy at once *global, forward deployed,* and *superior* to our probable opponents. Global, because our interests, allies, and opponents are global; forward deployed, because to protect those interests and allies, and to deter those opponents, we must be where they are; superior, because if deterrence fails it is better to win than lose.

But do we have the correct strategy? Today's debates would benefit from a more precise understanding of the role of strategy. Strategy is not a formula for fighting each ship and deploying each tank in the battles that

At left, exceptional shiphandling is required for safe personnel transfers between ships underway. Many a sailor, from seaman to admiral, have been "dipped" while highlining.

may take place around the world. That is not the function of the military establishment inside the Washington Beltway. Such is the proper function only of the theater commander who is given the responsibility to carry out the defense objectives set by the national command authorities.

Beyond the central concept of global, forward-deployed, and superior naval forces, strategy's role is to give coherence and direction to the process of allocating money among competing types of ships and aircraft and different accounts for spare parts, missile systems, defense planning, and the training of forces. It provides guidelines to aid us in allocating both resources and shortages.

Title 10 of the U.S. Code charges the Secretary of the Navy with ensuring the highest level of training appropriate to the resposibilities placed upon both the Marine Corps and the Navy. That is what strategy provides to us—a framework within which to train. For example, U.S. naval forces recently conducted a major training exercise, "Ocean Safari 85," with our NATO allies and the U.S. Coast Guard and Air Force. The "Safari" assembled off the East Coast of the United States and fought its way across the Atlantic, moved north of England and east of Iceland, and ended up in the Norwegian Sea. Approximately 155 ships and 280 fixed-wing aircraft and helicopters operated for four weeks in this environment, against 19 real Soviet ships and submarines and 96 Soviet aircraft sorties.

That is very effective training, and it is being carried out as part of a coherent training operational plan—linked to the way that the theater commanders intend to fight a war. One will search in vain, however, for a Navy cookbook that tells those on-scene commanders when to

move aircraft carriers, or how or where to move attack submarines or Aegis cruisers at any given point after a conflict commences. There should never be any such cookbook and certainly it should never come from Washington. Those who criticize our strategy for being the wrong cookbook or for not having a cookbook do not understand strategy.

Other critics argue that our Navy should be less global, less forward-deployed, or less superior with the resources saved to be poured into a stronger continental defense. To be less global means to abandon some area of our vital interests. To believe that in the case of the Northern Flank of NATO, for example, a "passive" defense line thrown across the Greenland-Iceland-United Kingdom Gap will somehow protect our sea lanes or defer an engagement with Soviet forces demonstrates a lack of understanding of the fundamental mechanics of war at sea and the workings of NATO and the Soviets' own operational requirements. No coalition of free nations can survive a

strategy which begins by sacrificing its more exposed allies to a dubious military expediency. To suggest that naval support of Norway or Turkey is too dangerous because it must be done close to the Soviet Union is defeatist. To suggest that such a strategy is provocative of the Soviets just indicates the lengths to which some critics will go, in order to portray Soviet intentions as solely defensive.

As for strengthening our continental defenses, we and our allies are also doing just that. To discard maritime superiority in an attempt to match the larger Soviet ground forces, however, would give us neither conventional deterrence on land nor secure access by sea unless the Western democracies are prepared to militarize their societies to an unprecedented, and unwise, degree.

Because research and development projects span decades, and ships take many years to build, the makeup of our fleet can not change radically with each administration. Instead, the fleet evolves over time with policy and technology. The fleet today reflects the

Tank landing ships, like the one at left, offload cargo and vehicles by means of a 112-foot ramp over their bow; below, the Spruance-class destroyer USS O'Brien, approaches an aircraft carrier.

wisdom of the deck plates, the labs, and lessons learned from our exercises. The size and design of our ships and weapons reflect the inputs of sailors in contact with Soviet "Victor" submarines, *Kiev*-class carriers and "Bear" aircraft. The wisdom of common sense and the highest available technology are tremendous advantages, brought to the design of today's Navy and Marine Corps.

Of course, there are many kinds of ships not in the fleet today that could do very well. The British *Invincible*-class vertical or short take-off and landing (VSTOL) carriers are quite capable antisubmarine warfare ships. It would be nice to have some of them in the U.S. Navy. There are many attractive European frigate designs, and we could make good use of them. There are also diesel submarines in our European alliance navies that fulfill very effective roles.

If the taxpayers of our allies around the world were not buying these vessels, the burden would fall upon us.

But happily, they are carrying a considerable share of the cost of naval defense and American taxpayers do not have to fund a Navy greater than about 600 ships.

Perhaps the most debated issue on newspapers' front pages and television talk shows is whether our aircraft carriers should be large or small. There is no absolute answer to this question, but in my view, the evidence still seems overwhelmingly in favor of the *Nimitz* (CVN-68)-class carrier of 90,000 tons as the optimum size and design for putting air capability at sea.

Could we gainfully employ more mid-size carriers like our 64,000-ton *Midway* (CV-41) and *Coral Sea* (CV-43)? Yes, indeed. They would be very useful. The Navy would like to have five more of them if we could afford to buy them. At least, we will keep these two smaller carriers steaming in the force for a long time to come.

Similarly, with our nuclear attack submarines, we could buy more of them if we compromised on their

capabilities. But our tremendous edge in technology is a permanent potential built into the nature of our culture and our economic system compared with the Soviets. We must build to this advantage, and not trade it away for cheaper, smaller, less capable ships built in greater numbers, which is the forte of a totalitarian, centralized, Gosplan economy.

It would be a great mistake for us to adopt a defense strategy at sea—any more than on land—that attempts to match totalitarian regimes in sheer numbers of cheap reproducible items. Time and again, the high-tech solution has proved to be the wisest investment, and by far the most advantageous one for the United States and its allies. This is true of our missiles, our aircraft, and our ships. We have the world's finest fighting equipment.

So we are getting the "right" Navy. Although there are plenty of other kinds of ships we would like to have, and we could certainly use the larger Navy long advocated by the Joint Chiefs, we have stayed consistently with the 600-ship fleet because we are prepared to bet that our allies will continue to maintain modern, effective navies and air forces. We are prepared to accept the risk that our nation will make the right decisions to prevent losses of forces early in a conflict, and we think that that is a prudent risk to run in order to have an affordable Navy.

Can We Afford the Navy This Nation Needs?

Numerous studies and surveys, among them a tome by the Congressional Budget Office, suggest that we cannot afford to sustain, or properly man, a 600-ship Navy. Just the reverse is true. Consider the facts. We have now, under construction and fully funded, *all* of the ships necessary to attain a 600-ship Navy centered on 15 carrier battle groups, four battleship surface action groups, and 100 nuclear-powered attack submarines.

Our long-term plans in a "zero growth" budget for fiscal year 1986 now reflect reductions in our shipbuilding and aircraft procurement programs. These reductions will be to levels we call the sustaining rate for the 600-ship Navy, an average 20 ships a year in new construction. The actual number will be higher or lower in a given year, depending on the block obsolescence of various types of ships.

The 20-ship average is a sound basis for planning, in part because of improved maintenance and the corresponding increase in longevity. Instead of the average 26 years of life that we realized from our ships in the 1960s and the 1970s, we are now getting 30 years' service from our ships, because of better maintenance,

At left, it's hot work in the engine room of the aircraft carrier *USS John F. Kennedy*; top, a sparrow missile is launched from JFK; an A-7E Corsair II launches from *USS America*; midshipmen train aboard the fleet oiler *USS Willamette*.

Flattop Nauticabilia

F-14 A Tomcat

Total Cost:	Approx. $3.1 billion
Propulsion:	Nuclear power; only needs refueling after 15 years of normal operation
Speed:	More than 30 knots
Number of Reactors:	Two
Length of Flight Deck:	1,092 feet
Breadth of Flight Deck:	252 feet
Area of Flight Deck:	4.5 acres
Number of Aircraft Elevators:	Four
Number of Aircraft Catapults:	Four
Height, Keel to Mast:	244 feet (equal to a 24 story building)

F/A-18 Hornet

Compartments and Spaces:	3,360
Anchors:	Two, weighing 30 tons each
Weight of Anchor Chain Link:	360 pounds each
Combat Load Displacement:	95,000 tons (190 million pounds; equivalent to the weight of 47,500 cars)
Accommodations:	Approx. 6,200
Airplanes and Helicopters:	Approx. 100
Propellers:	Four (Each is 21 feet tall and weighs 66,200 pounds)
Number of Telephones:	More than 2,000
Weight of Rudders:	65.5 tons each
Capacity of Air Conditioning:	2,520 tons (Enough to serve more than 800 homes)
Daily Capacity of Distilling Plants:	400,000 gallons (Enough for daily needs of 2,000 homes)
Total Ouptut of Electronic Equipment:	Equal to output of about 50 broadcasting stations, operating simultaneously
Estimated Number of Tubes, Transistors and Diodes:	Over one billion
Number of Lighting Fixtures:	29,600
Length of Cable and Wiring:	Equal to 4,300 times the length of the ship
All Technical Manuals Aboard:	Stacked, they would be as high as the Washington Monument (555 feet)
Crew's Salary per Month:	Approx. $900,000.00
Number of Meals Served Daily:	18,150
Average Daily Consumption:	10,000 eggs 10,000 pancakes 2,700 pounds of meat Too much coffee

E-2C Hawkeye

SH-3H Sea King

H-46 Sea Knight

S-3A Viking

EA-6B Prowler

the absence of a big backlog of overhauls, and the higher technology that we are putting into our ships.

This "good news" should not blind us to the requirements of the future. A steady 20-new-ships-a-year average will require 3% budget growth. A future of zero-growth budgets would mean that we will be unable to sustain a 600-ship Navy—or for that matter, a capable defense. We know from painful experience in the 1970s that the damage done by no-growth funding is far greater than the mere percentage budget loss would indicate. With zero- or negative-growth budgets, the industrial infrastructure vital to fleet construction and support shrinks dramatically. The result is a loss in competitive bidding and a return to sole-sourced monopolies. Rates of production must then be cut, individual unit costs increase dramatically, productivity falls, and, in the final accounting, the American taxpayer gets much less "bang for the buck." Even worse is the decline in the quality and morale of the people who man the fleet, as we saw in the late 1970s.

Is 3% real growth beyond our means? Throughout the past two decades, many commentators favoring a reduced defense effort have repeatedly predicted that the American people will not support sustained defense growth. That refrain is now put forward by some, including the Congressional Budget Office, as a fact of life. While it may express their hopes, it is not supported by history. That view takes as its norm the flat or even declining figures of the immediate post-Vietnam War period. In fact, except for those years, post-World War II naval budgets maintained growth commensurate with our national economy. The middle and late Seventies, by contrast, are now being seen as an anomaly in U.S. history. It is not apparent, the Congressional Budget Office notwithstanding, that the American people wish to "restore" that aberrant pattern of declining numbers of ships, morale, and readiness.

In procurement, we should not assume that Congress will refuse to make the necessary legislative changes in the way we in the Department of the Navy are permitted to conduct our business. Indeed, I suggest that, in the current aura of public concern over budget deficits and government spending, there would be few more cost-effective and money-saving moves that Congress could undertake than the removal of excessive regulations and red tape that characterize the environment in which the Navy operates today. For example, there repose in the Library of Congress today no less than 1,152 linear feet of statutory and regulatory law governing procurement alone! That is the *real* Washington Monument!

Along with over-regulation, we are faced with excessive, layered bureaucracies, and the accretion of authority without concomitant responsibility into a confusing labyrinth of congressional oversight committees and federal agencies without end, creating tremendous inefficiencies.

Top left, USO shows bring welcome relief from long deployments; bottom left, Navy SEALs train in the Pacific Ocean off Coronado, California; above, helos huddled like a covey of quail aboard the amphibious assault ship *USS Saipan*.

Breathing Life Into Ships

WHEN THE BUILDERS have finished with a new ship she is still an inanimate thing. Her hull is seaworthy, her engines are sound, and her gear is good, but you can't tell whether she is destined to become a proud and respected lady, or a weak sister.

When her crew steps aboard, the ship comes to life. The skipper, the officers, and each man in her crew, all loan her a piece of their souls, to keep as long as they serve in her. These little pieces added together make up the soul of the ship and change her from so many tons of cold metal to a warm, living and breathing member of the seagoing community of ships.

Some people think, that despite all our modern scientific knowledge, man will never learn how to put life into inanimate matter. Seafaring men have been doing this for centuries.

Daniel V. Gallery
Rear Admiral, U.S. Navy (Retired)

For dock landing ship *USS Fort McHenry*, bright sunshine and colorful balloons guarantee a festive commissioning ceremony.

U.S. Navy Battle Force Silhouettes

USS Nimitz, aircraft carrier; 90,944 tons; 1,092 feet; 3,136 complement; 2,800 air wing

USS Iowa, battleship; 58,000 tons; 887.2 feet; 1,518 complement

USS Ticonderoga, Aegis cruiser; 9,600 tons; 565.8 feet; 358 complement

USS Tarawa, amphibious assault ship; 39,300 tons; 820 feet; 935 complement; 1,700 troops

USS Kidd, guided missile destroyer; 8,300 tons; 563 feet; 339 complement

USS Spruance, destroyer; 7,810 tons; 563 feet; 319 complement

USS Samuel Gompers, destroyer tender; 20,500 tons; 644 feet; 1,681 complement

USS Ohio, ballistic missile submarine; 18,700 tons; 560 feet; 155 complement

USS Whidbey Island, dock landing ship; 15,726 tons; 609 feet; 340 complement; 450 troops

USS Newport, tank landing ship; 8,450 tons; 522 feet; 257 complement; 400 troops

USS California, guided missile cruiser; 10,450 tons; 596 feet; 603 complement

USS Oliver Hazard Perry, guided missile frigate; 3,585 tons; 445 feet; 206 complement

USS Cimarron, fleet oiler; 26,110 tons; 592 feet; 217 complement

USS Bronstein, frigate; 2,650 tons; 371.5 feet; 216 complement

USS Avenger, mine countermeasure ship; 1,040 tons; 224 feet; 72 complement

USS Los Angeles, attack submarine; 6,927 tons; 360 feet; 133 complement

USS Pegasus, patrol combatant missile (hydrofoil); 239.6 tons; 132.9 feet; 24 complement

USS Austin, amphibious transport dock; 16,914 tons; 570 feet; 420 complement; 930 troops

The Congressional Budget Office staffers and others who look at the Navy's future costs assume that just because this bloated, inefficient congressional executive system has been in place it will *remain* in place. I do not accept that. Moreover, we have shown in the Navy an historic reversal of the trend of inevitable cost increases.

Today, for example, the last contract that we signed for a follow-on Aegis cruiser was $900 million. Four years ago, these cruisers cost more than $1.2 billion each, and were projected to reach $1.6 billion by the end of 1985. It did not happen, though, because we brought competition into the program. Both producing yards brought in new efficiencies and instituted strict cost discipline, while we in the Navy applied a new asceticism to our gold-plating lusts. All of our shipbuilding programs show the same pattern. We have gone from only 24% competition in 1981 to 90% competition in 1985, producing an average of $1 billion in cost *under*runs for each of the last four years.

Contrary to what the nay-sayers predicted, the costs of Navy aircraft have been going down, not up. This is a sea change, a break with 30 years of uninterrupted cost escalation in naval aircraft procurement. During 1976-1981, growth in aircraft unit prices averaged about 10% in constant fiscal year 1980 dollars. In 1981, we implemented vigorous cost management programs which emphasized competition, no design changes, and firm fixed-price contracts. These efforts have paid off in reduced aircraft prices every since 1982.

For example, we reached agreement with McDonnell Douglas on a fiscal year 1985 fly-away price of $18.7 million for the F/A-18 strike fighter. In terms of fiscal year 1982 dollars, this is a price 32% below that paid in

The trident strategic missile submarine *USS Michigan* is towed into the magnetic silencing facility at Bangor, Washington. Top right, two F/A-18 Hornets maneuver during a Blue Angels air show; below right, a CH-46 Sea Knight helicopter launches.

Above, on U.S. Navy ships, boxing "smokers" are popular during holidays at sea. Aboard *USS Fairfax County*, two shipmates provide the crew with welcome diversion from the work routine. Clockwise from lower left: a technician pours over schematics aboard the AEGIS cruiser *USS Bunker Hill*; aviation mechanics are one of many career fields open to Navy women; an F-14 Tomcat is launched from the carrier *USS Theodore Roosevelt*; firefighting drill aboard *USS Bunker Hill*; a sailor exits the submarine *USS Guardfish*; port bow view of the hospital ship *USNS Mercy*.

1982. Purchases in 1985 represent a savings to the taxpayer of $126 million for that year alone.

So, there is nothing inevitable about escalating costs and overruns in defense procurement. During the last four years we proved that it can be just as consistent to have underruns. And so if we just make prudent assumptions, not even optimistic assumptions, there is no question that we can maintain the size and the current mix of our force through the rest of this century with a 3% growth budget.

Just as significant, we can also maintain the tremendous turn-around in readiness that we have achieved with President Ronald Reagan's 7% growth budgets. During the past four years, the readiness of our ships and aircraft has increased nearly 40%. Even these statistics do not do justice to the palpable difference in the fleet itself, in morale, in readiness, and in safety — i.e., uncrashed airplanes and unbroken equipment and reduction of tragic accidents.

We know what we have accomplished during the past five years. Furthermore, we know we can maintain this record of success with the size budgets that are currently envisioned by the President.

The German military philosopher Clausewitz once observed that in the balance of power among nations, battle is to deterrence as cash is to credit in the world of commerce. One may live entirely by paper transactions *only* when there is no doubt about one's ability to settle accounts with hard currency when challenged.

Similarly, there must be no doubt in the minds of Soviet leaders that the United States and its allies can and will settle accounts, on both land and sea, if challenged. The 600-ship Navy is an essential element in this credibility. We *can*, and *must*, afford the naval power that will sustain the defense of this country's allies and interests around the world. ⊤

Navy Cross   Distinguished Flying Cross   Bronze Star   Congressional Medal of Honor

Top, an F-14 Tomcat at dusk; left, LT Pat Denkler was one of the first carrier qualified Navy women pilots; above, Navy's Blue Angels and Air Force Thunderbirds demonstrate aerobatic expertise.

*"The Lone Sailor...
represents all who have
served their country far from
home, in hardship and hazard."*

*"All Sailors live and survive
in the hostile and fickle
environment of the sea."*

IN WASHINGTON, D.C., on Pennsylvania Avenue, a statue has been erected in the open air. It is the figure of a man, seven feet high and made of bronze. His race, religion and ethnic origin are whatever we want them to be. He could be officer or enlisted, male or female. He could be active duty, a reservist, a civilian. The ocean could be any ocean, and the sailor could be standing on the fantail of a destroyer, in the engine room of a submarine, on the hangar deck of an aircraft carrier, or in any other special place where Navy people live and work.

In his expression there is a thoughtful look—of loneliness and yet of something more. He is thinking of home and of the pain of separation, the challenges that his family faces in making a life without him. But he is also thinking of the task at hand, the mission of his ship or squadron, the ideals of the great nation which he defends. He knows that each hour of his deployment across the oceans is an investment in that defense. And so his look is also one of purpose: excellent in his work, sure of himself and of his leaders, a man people count on, he radiates confidence and strength.

The Navy Memorial in Washington, with its Lone Sailor, was dedicated on October 13, 1987, the 212th anniversary of the founding of our service. In one sense, then, the sailor is new. But the qualities he represents, the values he defends, the sacrifices he makes, his communion with the sea—these are timeless, and all of you share in them, just as the millions share in them who have sailed and fought and died for them since 1775.

> C. A. H. Trost
> *Admiral, U.S. Navy*
> *Chief of Naval Operations*

THIS NAVY MEMORIAL is a living tribute to those millions of men and women who have served their country in the uniform of the United States Navy and been called "sailor." Through it's statuary and symbology, this Memorial stands for the traditions of the sea and it's people. It is representative of the global commitment of our Navy and it's people. It is the focal point for all of us who have gone down to the sea in ships, to look to in remembrance of the sacrifice that is made by all sailors. The long periods of separation from our loved ones; the deprivations resulting from extended periods at sea living in close quarters, often times in tense situations, never knowing if an unseen enemy will strike. Yet the fond memories are stimulated by this Memorial. The camaraderie of your shipmates. That common bond that ties all sailors to each other; the knowledge that you are doing something that is unique; that we live and survive in the hostile and fickle environment of the sea—one minute lulling you with it's serenity, and the next jolting you awake with it's violence.

Yes, this Memorial stands in recognition of the love of freedom cherished by sailors and the pride that runs through the being of all who willingly step forward, ready to make the ultimate sacrifice, in protecting that freedom, not only for themselves, but most importantly, for the preservation of the way of life in this great nation.

> William H. Plackett
> *Master Chief Petty Officer of the Navy*

THE DEDICATION of the United States Navy Memorial in Market Square Park is a major achievement in the revitalization of Pennsylvania Avenue.

From a historical perspective, the Memorial sits at the principal axis in Pierre L'Enfant's original plan for Washington—the important Eighth Street vista—and preserves the open space that L'Enfant had conceived for this site midway between the White House and the Capitol.

The Memorial and Park serve as a gateway to the Market Square neighborhood which is being restored at the eastern end of Pennsylvania Avenue.

Market Square Park/U.S. Navy Memorial is the result of a unique public-private partnership between PADC, a federal agency and the private U.S. Navy Memorial Foundation. The Foundation has funded key elements of the park including the design, the granite map of the world, the statue of the Lone Sailor and other sculpture, the flagpoles, and the Compass Rose. PADC funding has provided the special paving, landscaping, and lighting, and will create the glass-covered colonnade which has not yet been built. PADC and the Foundation have shared the cost of the fountains.

It is fitting that the men and women of the United States Navy should find a home on Pennsylvania Avenue, "America's Main Street." The Pennsylvania Avenue Development Corporation is proud to have joined with the U.S. Navy Memorial Foundation in bringing this project to completion.

Henry A. Berliner, Jr.
Chairman
Pennsylvania Avenue
Development Corporation

Wisdom from Davey Jones' Locker

WITH NEARLY THREE-QUARTERS of the earth's surface covered by water, it isn't surprising that volumes have been written about the world's waterways. When making reference to saltwater, the words "sea" and "ocean" are routinely used synonymously, even though geography reflects oceans to be much larger than seas.

According to *Peter Freuchen's Book of the Seven Seas*, the term "seven seas" dates back to ancient times, referring to the seas known to the Mohammedans before the 15th century. These were the Mediterranean, Red, China, East and West African Seas, the Persian Gulf and the Indian Ocean. More recently the poet Rudyard Kipling romanticized the "seven seas" by using the term in the title of a volume of his verse. To retain this now legendary number, the world's oceans are popularly divided into the Arctic, North and South Pacific, North and South Atlantic, Indian and Antarctic Oceans. Interestingly, the International Hydrographic Bureau, located in Monaco, doesn't recognize the existence of an Antarctic Ocean.

President John Adams once wrote, "Neither nature nor art has partitioned the sea into empires. The ocean and its treasures are the common property of all men. Upon this deep and strong foundation do I build, and with this cogent and irresistible argument do I fortify our rights and liberties."

Continuing the semantics—the International Hydrographic Bureau lists 54 seas--some are seas within seas. For example, within the Mediterranean Sea are listed seven smaller bodies of water also categorized as seas. Technically then, a landlubbing, not so salty, "Old Salt," could claim to have sailed the "seven seas" without ever passing the Rock of Gibraltar, through the Dardenelles or transiting the Suez Canal.

This leads me to one final quote by the author Joseph Conrad: "And now the old ships and their men are gone; the new ships and the new men, many of them bearing the old auspicious names, have taken up their watch on the stern and impartial sea which offers no opportunities but to those who know how to grasp them with a ready hand and an undaunted heart."

—JWA

Ready for Anything

*Renowned novelist Herman Wouk was honored
as the first recipient of the "Lone Sailor Award,"
at a U.S. Navy Memorial Dinner on June 23,
1987. Upon accepting the award statuette, the
author made this extemporaneous response.*

ALLOW ME TO BEGIN by quoting a few words from my
novel, *War and Remembrance.*

Vice Admiral Victor Henry, long retired, is writing an
article about the Battle of Leyte Gulf for the Naval Institute
Proceedings. This is what he writes:

> *"The Battle of Leyte Gulf stands as a monument to
> the subhuman stupidity of warfare in our age of
> science and industry. The time for war is over. As
> the human race has outgrown human sacrifice,
> human slavery, and dueling, it has to outgrow war.
> The means now dwarf the results, and destructive
> machinery has become a senseless resort in politics."*

So far, what Pug Henry says would be accepted by all
those disenchanted with the military, and appalled by the
nuclear bind in which we find ourselves, toward the end of
the twentieth century.

But then Pug Henry—who speaks here in my voice—
adds a few words which perhaps make me something of a
Lone Sailor in postwar literature. Here is how he
concludes.

> *Yet, while belligerent fools or villains anywhere on
> earth consider war an optional policy, what can free
> men do but confront them with what met the
> Japanese at Leyte Gulf and Adolph Hitler in the skies
> over England in 1940—daunting force, and self-
> sacrificing brave spirits ready to wield it?"*

The Lone Sailor is one of those self-sacrificing brave
spirits. I know him well.

I saw him on the forecastle as we approached an
invasion beach in the dawn, in his kapok jacket and his
steel helmet, at his battle station by the number one gun,
ready for anything that would come.

I saw him in the wheelhouse and in the radar shack
during a typhoon, when our old minesweeper was rolling
40 or 45 degrees, standing by his station and doing his job.

I saw the Lone Sailor, as you see him in this statue, on
the forecastle as we steamed homeward for a navy yard
overhaul, passing from the warm South Pacific to the
cold December waters off Northern California; his
hands jammed in his peajacket pockets, his eyes gazing
toward the Golden Gate and toward home.

But if I know him, and I think I do, the Lone Sailor
looks beyond the shores of battle and the shoes of home
to a distant shore, and to the quintessence of the
American dream. He looks to the day when *"the nation
will not lift up sword against nation, neither will they
learn war anymore."*

Until that distant day comes, he stands at his station,
ready to do this job. And, I think it is because I have
spoken up for him that you give me this most moving
honor; because in truth you are honoring him, the Lone
Sailor.

Author Herman Wouk with Chairman, Joint
Chiefs of Staff Admiral William Crowe, Jr.

Reflections by the Top Sailor

WILLIAM H. PLACKETT

Master Chief Petty Officer of the Navy

THE ESSENCE OF THE UNITED STATES NAVY is her people. It is therefore appropriate that the center piece of this fine memorial be the statue of the Lone Sailor. This single figure, with his seabag at his feet, embodies all things that we stand for. But who is this Lone Sailor? Where does he come from? What does he feel? What does he stand for? These and many other questions must be answered to truly depict the heart and soul of our great Navy.

This sailor is hometown America. He represents the men and women who come from throughout this great nation. They are the products of the inner city, the small town, the farms and wetlands of America. They are from college town USA, from steel mills, coal mines or may have been watermen. They are from our heart. They come together from diverse geographic and cultural backgrounds and through shared experience, become a homogenous group prepared to face any adversity that may confront them in their defense of our country.

This Lone Sailor stands for many things to many people. His significance is in the eyes of the beholder. To the average citizen he represents the fun loving, rambunctious young man or woman next door who has gone off to seek adventure and see the world. He is the symbol of the Navy—the young man in a tailored set of dress blues with his hands thrust deep into his peacoat

pockets, his hat square, but yet with a slight cock to it. A stance that one could assume to be belligerent, but we all know is borne of the endless hours bent into the wind during topside watches. The slight set of the hat over the right or left eye that could be mistaken for brash cockiness, but yet we know to be a result of confidence in self and service. And that certain walk that could be perceived as a swagger, but we know to be a result of one part bracing against the roll and pitch of the deck and one part pride. All these attitudes combine to exemplify those attributes of pride, confidence and self assuredness shared by all men of the sea.

To the young woman with a baby in her arms and one at her hem, this Lone Sailor represents the absent husband who has chosen the sea as his profession. He represents the guy who periodically goes away for extended periods of time, creating that great sense of loss that engulfs her heart as he stands forlornly at the rail of his ship waving goodbye. This is the one who puts her through hell each time he deploys, but can erase all those hours of loneliness with a shy smile when he returns. He is her knight on the back of a haze grey charger off to defeat the enemy. This Sailor is the person whose arms provided a sanctuary for her and their children. He is the person in her life who can make her angry in a flash, but can immediately extinguish the flames of that anger with a small smile at the corner of his mouth and an abashed look in his eye. He is the man she loves and the father of her children. The women who become Navy wives are a unique breed themselves. They are ladies who have confidence and tenacity to watch that sailor leave, take care of all those things that must be done while we are gone without missing a beat,

WILLIAM H. PLACKETT is the sixth Master Chief Petty Officer of the Navy (MCPON). This office was formally established on March 1st, 1967, to provide a direct, unofficial channel of communications between enlisted personnel and the senior policy levels of the Department of the Navy. The MCPON is the senior enlisted advisor to the Chief of Naval Operations on all matters pertaining to enlisted personnel.

and then when we return have the ability to make us feel as though we were truly missed. That takes a special person to do those things, and no discussion of the Navy can be complete without the proper tribute to those we leave behind. They are truly special people.

To the older lady staring wistfully into the past as she surveys the Memorial, this Lone Sailor perhaps stands for the husband or son whom she has sent off to war, never to return.

To all sailors who have served, we see ourselves in the Lone Sailor. We see symbolically what we all remember ourselves to have been. No matter how dim our vision has become, or how much water has gone under the keel, we will always remember ourselves in that way. Forthright, standing tall, ready to accept any challenge that might come our way. We see the spirit that permeates our people. The spirit of patriotism that—regardless of whether or not we would admit it to our shipmates—runs just beneath our skin and deep in our heart. The spirit that has motivated sailors for

Top, despite sophisticated communications systems, ships still "talk" to one another using Morse code and signal lights and, center, colorful signal flags stored in a "flag bag; at right, sextants provide a valuable back-up for electronic navigation systems.

generations to live on the edge—to seek adventure wherever they may be—at sea or ashore on liberty. The Lone Sailor also brings to mind the pride we all share in the uniform we wear and what it stands for. The pride and sense of accomplishment that comes from knowing that you have challenged and survived in an environment that can be as compelling as the smile of a beautiful woman, or as savage as a violent beast. The simple pleasures that mean so much to men of the sea also come to mind. The sharing of an evening bull session on the fantail, watching the florescent wake under a sky filled with a moon that is larger than life and a sky full of stars close enough to reach out and touch. The camaraderie borne of a companionship among shipmates developed through common experience and sharing. Friendships that are woven of a fabric so strong that it cannot be rendered. The closeness of shipmates cannot be explained to those who have not shared the experience. That bond that results from long periods away from those we love, arduous working conditions that run the gamut from the freezing cold of a north Atlantic topside watch to the oppressive heat of the hole. The wild swing of emotion one endures, from the total depression of departure to the elation of the

homecoming; the dejection one suffers when a mail call does not produce a letter, or pictures of a growing child that tear at your heart and bring tears to the eye. That sense of satisfaction and pride in unit that results from a simple "atta-boy" from the battle group or fleet commander. And some guilt—because we are off doing all the neat things we do as Navymen while the one we have left behind must cope with the broken plumbing or a car that won't start, and children who demand and deserve so much love and attention from both parents. These are the things we share as sailors. These are the foundations on which our friendships are built. They are common to all sailors, and are the memories stimulated by the Lone Sailor.

To the young man or woman just starting out, the Lone Sailor stands as a figure to which they look to, and holds the mystique of adventure and excitement of being a sailor, ever vigilant, ever ready.

This Memorial, then, is about people, the officers and crew who make up the Navy. The Lone Sailor stands as a mute sentinel, forever guarding the shores of our island nation to ensure that the freedom of the country that our forefathers forged out of a wilderness will forever remain intact. He stands as representative of the hundreds of thousands of sailors who are at sea around the world, separated from peace and war only by the sound of the general quarters alarm, to protect all of those things that are guaranteed by our constitution and our democracy. To have it said of a man, "He is a good sailor," implies so much that there can be no greater tribute. The Lone Sailor is a memorial to all "good sailors." ⚓

A Navy for Tomorrow

Rear Admiral J.B. "Brad" Mooney, Jr., USN (Ret.)

Former Chief of Naval Research

The birth of the Navy during the American Revolution was by no means glorious. When the patriots started shooting, April 19, 1775, they gave little thought to forming any Navy at all. They were concerned only with "Redcoats," who were soldiers, not sailors.

The need for a naval force became clear, however, when the British Navy showed its strength by stopping up the colonial harbors. Even then, the 13 colonies, though united in purpose, were generally divided in their opinions of what a Navy should be.

After much deliberation, on October 13, 1775, delegates to the Continental Congress approved only by a very narrow majority a proposal to establish a Navy by authorizing the arming of a single "swift, sailing vessel."

Gradually, the young Continental Navy Fleet grew larger though hardly a real match for the Royal Navy. Most American warships were modified privateers and makeshift gunboats, manned by officers and sailors who were either ill-prepared or ill-suited for naval warfare. It was not an auspicious beginning.

Despite the initial chaos, however, the new Navy was not ill-fated. Seapower became an important part of the colonies' struggle for independence, and the Navy, born of hard necessity, was to become an important part of the new nation. It is a tribute to its leaders and something called "Yankee ingenuity" that the Continental Navy prevailed.

A lot has happened since then, both in the United States and in its Navy, as any examination of national or naval history reveals. History also reveals that the progress of the U.S. Navy has directly paralleled the progress of the country and the people it serves. The common progress began with an early recognition of the value of science. Science shaped inventions, inventions shaped technology, and technology shaped the history of the republic.

It was one of America's first scientist-inventors, Benjamin Franklin, who helped bring the Continental Navy up to par with the British Navy during the War of Independence. One reason he was sent to France was to buy better ships, inasmuch as French ships were bigger and better armed than any the colonies could build. American shipwrights simply lacked the technology to design fighting ships like those in the British fleet. Under Franklin's influence, France and her warships helped the Americans balance the scales. One of those French ships was renamed *Bon Homme Richard* by Captain John Paul Jones, in honor of Franklin's "Poor Richard."

A Connecticut Yankee's Turtle

The Continental Navy did not have to rely on foreign technology alone. The Navy started using "Yankee ingenuity" even before Franklin went to France. It started in 1775 when David Bushnell, a Yale medical student, thought of a way to sink British warships with an undersea boat which would attach a torpedo to their hulls. His invention was called the "Marine Turtle," described by Bushnell as having "some resemblance to two upper tortoise shells of equal size, joined together. . ."

Not quite eight feet long, and six feet high, the "Turtle" could be propelled by its single operator at about three knots under ideal conditions. After

Rear Admiral John Bradford Mooney, Jr. is a Naval Academy graduate who spent 34 years in the sea service. His assignments included command of a submarine, Oceanographer of the Navy and Chief of Naval Research.

A Yale medical student named David Bushnell designed the first submarine for warfare, "Turtle," to drive the British out of New York Harbor.

demonstrating the seaworthiness of his apparatus before Governor Trumbull of Connecticut, Bushnell and the "Turtle" were shipped off to New York in September 1776 to try it on the British Fleet in harbor there. The plan was to arm the "Turtle" with an oak casing filled with 150 pounds of explosives, maneuver the partially submerged "Turtle" along side an enemy ship and, with an auger, attach the charge to the ship's bottom and detonate the charge by a simple clockwork mechanism. A Connecticut Militia volunteer, Sergeant Ezra Lee, made the attempt, but was unable to penetrate the copper hull of the British ship and attach the explosive as planned. Nevertheless, one of Bushnell's "torpedoes" went off which worried the British into transferring their station ships to the outer bay.

As unsuccessful as the "Turtle" was in combat, it represented an important contribution to naval engineering as the first practical submarine and the first screw-propelled vessel. It was also a pioneer in mine and torpedo warfare. With the "Turtle," the Navy's association with science and invention was off to a very good start.

Humphreys' Grand Design

During the period immediately following the Revolution, the Americans gave almost all their attention to the new Constitution, and the Continental Navy was demobilized in 1785 by an economy-minded

Congress. But the dormancy of American seapower had lasted barely a decade when President George Washington persuaded the Congress in 1794 to authorize a new naval force to combat the growing menace of piracy on the high seas.

The heart of the new United States Navy was in six frigates of a bold, new design conceived by a Philadelphia Quaker named Joshua Humphreys, whose ideas Washington had sought. Humphreys' reply to the President is another testament to American ingenuity:

As our Navy for a considerable time will be inferior in numbers, we are to consider what size ships will be most formidable and be an overmatch for those of an enemy. . . Frigates will be the first object, and none ought to be built less than 150 feet keel, to carry 30 24-pounders on the gun-deck. Ships of this construction have everything in their favor; their great length gives them the advantage of sailing, which is an object of the first magnitude. They are superior to any European frigate, and if others be in company, our frigates can always lead ahead and never be obliged to go into action but on their own terms, except in a calm. . .

Humphreys' plans were a major departure from the standard designs of France and England, but so was the new form of constitutional government. His ships were built and launched in 1797 as the first vessels of the U.S. Navy. Among them were the *United States*, the *Constellation*, and the *Constitution*—even the names were characteristically American. They were everything Humphreys had promised, and more. Their place in naval history was unwittingly predicted by Admiral Lord Nelson when he saw the *Constitution*, later known as "Old Ironsides," put into Gibraltar after the American victory over the Barbary pirates in 1804. He said, "In the handling of those transatlantic ships there is a nucleus of trouble for the Navy of Great Britain." There was, indeed.

A Spirit of Innovation

The United States fought its second war with England with a few technical advantages. The Royal Navy was still acknowledged best in the world in 1812, but the U.S. Navy had some elements of surprise on its side. Americans had learned much since the first war. Their previous naval weaknesses—ships, ordnance and men—had been neutralized by the new frigates, heavier, sighted cannon and better-disciplined crews. These advantages were the result of innovations the British knew little about, and helped the U.S. Navy to stand up to a numerically larger fleet.

Technical innovations continued during the war— again out of necessity—and American ships became even better. The impetus allowed the U.S. Navy in 1814 to become the first in the world to launch a warship without sails: the steam-powered *Demologos*, designed and built by Robert Fulton. The Navy had become part of the age of invention.

The spirit of innovation born during the American Revolution became firmly fixed in the Navy during the Industrial Revolution. American seapower in the 19th century grew step by step with American technology. Steam replaced sail. Screw replaced paddlewheel. Iron replaced wood. Technology brought new problems, also, and in an effort to solve them the Navy developed a greater interest in the basic knowledge that made the technical improvements possible. They needed to *know* more. For example, the Navy needed to know how to build boilers that would not explode from steam pressure, or how to get more speed and power from ships weighted down with iron. Science had the answers, and Navy men were clearly visible wherever scientific work was being done.

Adams and Wilkes, Pioneers

Some credit is due President John Quincy Adams for the Navy's interest in science. As an outspoken advocate of government support of scientific enterprise, he encouraged official military participation in it. Three of his more emphatic proposals were eventually accepted and placed under Navy direction many years after his term expired:

- In 1825, President Adams urged Congress to establish a Naval Academy "for the formation of scientific and accomplished officers." The academy was established at Annapolis, Maryland, in 1845, with no less than half of its curriculum devoted to science and engineering.
- Adams also proposed the creation of a national astronomical observatory to match Europe's "lighthouses of the skies," but he could get no Congressional support. Such an observatory evolved, however, out of the Navy Depot of Charts and Instruments set up by the Secretary of the Navy in 1830 to care for chronometers, charts and other navigational equipment. In 1844, the Depot in Washington, D.C., became the U.S. Naval Observatory, the first scientific institution the Navy could call its own.
- In 1828, Adams suggested a coastal exploration of the northwest frontier to add to the important knowledge gained by Lewis and Clark. Ten years later, after much political maneuvering, a national scientific expedition departed for the Pacific Ocean led by Navy Lieutenant Charles Wilkes.

The Wilkes Expedition bears further discussion because it represents an important milestone in the history of federal support of science. During the 19th century, westward expansion and the growth of international trade demanded knowledge of distant regions. Unfortunately, owners of merchant ships were not equipped to finance expensive voyages of discovery. But Navy ships were already traveling to distant ports, if only for diplomatic or military reasons.

Congressmen were persuaded that exploration would be in the government's best interest, so Congress authorized, and President Andrew Jackson approved, the United States Exploring Expedition in May 1836. Besides a direct appropriation of $150,000, the bill provided authority to use matching funds from the Navy Department.

After two years of fitful preparation, the expedition was finally organized by Joel Roberts Poinsett, Secretary of War under President Martin Van Buren. He gave it an exclusively scientific mission, "to extend the bounds of human knowledge," and selected a commanding officer with more scientific background than rank (LT Wilkes, at the time, was the director of the Depot of Charts and Instruments). Poinsett also allowed Navy specialists in hydrography, mapping, and magnetic and astronomical observation to join the civilian scientists on the voyage.

For four years they explored a wide area of the Pacific Ocean, touching the Antarctic, Latin America, the Central Pacific Islands and the western coast of North America. They brought back valuable knowledge in the sciences of anthropology, botany, ethnology, geology, hydrography, meteorology, physics and zoology. In addition, the survey resulted in many navigational charts, some of which were used by the Navy at Tarawa in 1943. The results of the Wilkes Expedition greatly enhanced the scientific stature of the United States, and its Navy, in the world. Those results also introduced the Navy to the value of pure or basic science, which up to that time had been subordinated to practical or applied science.

Charting a New Science

Stimulated by the success of Wilkes' Expedition, overseas exploration dominated scientific activity in the 1840's and 50's, and the Navy played a prominent role. While the country was expanding westward, naval officers led expeditions to West Africa, the Middle East, Central and South America, the China Sea and Japan, and the North Pacific Ocean, gathering more

information to add to the growing American storehouses of scientific knowledge. While these Navy explorers were collecting knowledge *at* sea, a shore-based Navy lieutenant was collecting knowledge *about* the sea, much of it indirectly provided by the explorers themselves.

Matthew Fontaine Maury became the director of the Depot of Charts and Instruments in 1842, continuing as superintendent when the Depot became the U.S. Naval Observatory. As such, however, he was more interested in sea than sky and began collecting information on ocean currents and winds from the Navy's navigation charts. He also recorded and compared observations from naval and merchant ships' logs to form a comprehensive view of the world's oceans. He translated all his new data into practical guides for ocean navigation, publishing a series of *Wind and Current Charts* and *Sailing Directions* to help mariners to choose the most favorable routes. The immediate benefit of Maury's work was a significant reduction in average times of passage between ports for merchant ships. In fact, the clipper ships earned their reputation for speed with Maury's help. He even advised Cyrus Field on a suitable path for the transatlantic cable. Maury's systematic research had more scientific than commercial value, however. He gave organization to the science of marine physical geography, establishing him as the Navy's first oceanographer. Among his contributioins to the science was the first modern textbook in oceanography, *Physical Geography of the Sea.*

Technology Boom

By the time the Civil War began, military and naval technology had changed dramatically. There was a fourfold improvement in naval ships: steam engineering, screw propulsion, iron construction, and armor. Complementing these developments were changes in ordnance—the fused, explosive shell, the bottle-shaped Dahlgren gun, and slow-burning gunpowder. The improvements were not only in the use of these advances but also in the testing of them. Experimental testing replaced the hit-or-miss methods used before. The evaluation was scientific. It gave the Navy better control over the many technical innovations that modernized, yet complicated, its operations.

The sum of these innovations gave the industrial North an advantage over the agricultural South. Yet, it was the Confederate Navy that first made use of the ironclad warship. The rebel Navy built a kind of

inverted iron tub with sloping sides to cover the scuttled hull of the frigate *Merrimack* and renamed it the *CSS Virginia*. It was launched in March 1862, a day before its Union challenger was ready for an engagement.

The North had built an ironclad from a unique design by John Ericcson, who had earlier perfected the screw propeller. Christened the *Monitor*, Ericsson's ship was the product of several technological advances, including 40 patentable inventions like a revolving turret, ventilation and lighting systems, and an ammunition hoist. Designed as a total weapon system, the *Monitor* embodied the application of new technology to specific naval problems. It became the prototype for a new class of turreted ironclads. Again, it was war that made it necessary, but experimental science made it possible.

Scientists in Service

The Navy's use of science during the Civil War was fostered in part by civilian scientists. Early in 1862, Secretary of the Navy Gideon Welles set up a "permanent commission to which all subjects of a scientific character on which the government may require information may be referred." Members of the commission where Charles Henry Davis, first head of the Nautical Almanac; Alexander Bache, former head of the Coast Survey; and Joseph Henry, a prominent research scientist and secretary of the Smithsonian Institution.

The commission met frequently during the war, examining or testing not only inventions for new weapons but also new designs for ships. In addition, they set the stage for some lobbying by leading scientists of the day—Davis and Bache among them—to get Congressional approval for a National Academy of Sciences, an advisory body fashioned after England's Royal Society and the French Academy. The National Academy of Sciences was established with 50 members in March 1863 to "investigate, examine, experiment, and report upon any subject of science or art" for any government department. Four of the Academy's first five investigations concerned the Navy. The first committees were appointed:

- to consider ways to protect ships' hulls from salt water damage,
- to study the problems of calibrating compasses aboard iron ships,
- to evaluate an invention of a hydrometer, and
- to determine the worth of Maury's current charts and sailing directions.

The National Academy of Sciences created an official connection between the federal government and science, a connection fattened by a war fought with new technology. The U.S. Navy emerged from the Civil War as, perhaps, the best example of this new relation of science to technology, and the use that could be made of both. Unfortunately, it did not remain so.

The Boom is Lowered

The momentum of the industrial and technological revolution was not enough to keep science thriving in the Navy after the Civil War ended. It was not even enough to allow the Navy to keep the gains it had made. The improvements in ship construction, propulsion and ordnance were completely neutralized by postwar economic problems, public antipathy and political expediency. The chief blow dealt by the Navy hierarchy to progress was the reversion to wooden sailing ships in 1869, nullifying the important advances in steam engineering and metallurgy. The once formidable Union fleet of 670 ships shrank, and slowed, in the wake of bureaucratic ax-wielding. In 1874, the U.S. Navy consisted of a few dozen patched-up wooden cruisers, armed with smootbore, muzzle-loading guns, and manned by mercenary sailors and embarrassed officers. It was a match for few other navies in the world.

Star Attractions

The scientific function would have died completely during this period of decline except for a few naval activities that kept a spark alive. While most of the fleet was limping at sea, the Naval Observatory was studying the skies, and the Bureau of Navigation was surveying a piece of land.

With the establishment of a separate Hydrographic Office in 1866, the scientists at the Naval Observatory turned their full attention to astronomy. They began a new program of basic research in astronomy that was to give the Observatory renewed scientific prestige. Much of the program's merit came from the work of Simon Newcomb, a prominent mathematician who came to be regarded as one of the best American astronomers of the 19th century. Other noted scientists—Asaph Hall, George W. Hill and William Harkness—worked at the Observatory also. Together, these men made the Naval Observatory the national center of research in astronomical science during the final three decades of the 19th century. Their work was complemented by similar studies at the Nautical Almanac, which Newcomb directed from 1877 to 1897.

Ironclad Facts

A battleship can travel approximately eight feet on a gallon of fuel.

A battleship's 16-inch guns fire projectiles equivalent to lobbing Volkswagons 23 miles.

Exploration was another activity that helped science survive in the Navy during the fleet's postwar decline. During the period 1869-1874, the Bureau of Navigation conducted several surveys of Central American isthmus in order to examine possible routes for a canal between the Atlantic and Pacific Oceans. The surveys gathered enough information to determine the best route from an engineering standpoint.

Back on Course

The fleet's decline finally ended in the 1880's with the progressive policies of three successive Secretaries of the Navy. In 1881, Secretary William H. Hunt appointed a special board of officers to make recommendations about the Navy's needs. An obvious need was a better fleet, and they advised him to ask Congress to authorize 38 new cruisers and 25 new gunboats. Hunt barely finished asking before he became an ambassador, but he succeeded in conveying a sense of urgency over the Navy's plight.

In 1882, Secretary William E. Chandler extracted an appropriation for three cruisers and a dispatch boat. These were to be the first ships of a new Navy—steel-hulled, turreted and armed with new, high-powered, rifled guns. Congress also stipulated that the ships be built with domestic steel, giving a boost to the American steel industry. The new ships were delayed by technical problems which outlasted Secretary Chandler's term, but his successor, William C. Whitney, reaffirmed the need for modernizing the fleet. Whitney wrote in his annual report of 1885:

It is of little service to a nation to have any Navy at all unless it is a fair expression of the highest scientific resources of its day.

He squeezed an appropriation out of Congress for three more light cruisers, two armored cruisers and a torpedo boat. It was the beginning of a new fleet of "protected cruisers"—heavily armored and armed.

USS Iowa is one of four World War II battleships to be reactivated.

Along with the new ships came other innovations made possible by earlier experimentation. Work at the Naval Torpedo Station led to development of smokeless gunpowder. The torpedo was perfected. A few ships were equipped with electrical generators and lighting systems. Experiments with wireless telegraphy were made on board ship.

By 1890, the renewed growth of naval technology was gaining momentum. Public interest was revived and the Navy began to regain its strength. Between 1883 and 1892, the fleet grew by 26 ships, all but six of them armored. Three dozen more were added before the Spanish-American War, including the first four battleships and 17 high-speed torpedo boats.

The new U.S. Navy was combat-tested in 1898, and prevailed. The victory belonged to Navy men as well as ships, because they knew how to use the new technology more effectively by combining force with strategy. The officers had benefited from another improvement: better training in naval schools.

T. R. Builds a Fleet

One of the men responsible for American naval superiority was Theodore Roosevelt, Assistant Secretary of the Navy in 1897-98. When he was elected president in 1901, he sought to build up the Navy's power and make it as effective as possible. He was especially interested in new technology. For the Navy, he was in the right place at the right time. The period of his direct association with the Navy (1897-1909) was one of commitment to the "highest scientific resources of its day." A chronology:

1897—Internal combustion engine for use in the first submarine is demonstrated.

1898—Submarine *Holland* makes first dive. Roosevelt suggests Langley's "flying machine" be investigated. First hospital ship, *Solace,* outfitted; Hospital Corps established.

1899—Naval Model Basin for ship design opened.

1900—*USS Holland* commissioned. Marconi wireless devices installed in three ships; radio stations

Left and above: A Pioneer I remotely-piloted vehicle (RPV) is caught in a recovery net erected on the stern of the battleship *USS Iowa*. It is designed for basic gunfire support with over-the-horizon targeting and reconnaissance capabilities.

Off the coast of Venezuela, an F-14 Tomcat breaks the sound barrier.

erected in Washington and Annapolis to test transmission methods and equipment.

1902—Continuous-aim tracking for guns introduced.

1903—Naval Experiment Station and Testing Laboratory authorized by Congress. Naval Radio Station established at Navesink, N.J.

1904—Broadcasting of time originated at Navesink. Roosevelt assigns Navy major portion of government's use of radio; Navy has 33 ships and 18 shore stations equipped with radio.

1907—Bulbous-bow warship, *Delaware*, built on design of David Taylor to reduce ship resistance. "Great White Fleet" begins world cruise.

1908—Radio telephone used on board ship. Naval Radio Laboratory established.

With Roosevelt's active support, the Navy's attitude toward technological change remained positive. Naval ship design evolved from the turreted "monitors" through armored cruisers and torpedo bats to heavy battleships and fast destroyers. Important advantages were gained with improvements in firepower and propulsion. The Navy also focused its attention on new developments in aviation, submarines and radio.

By the time war had broken out in Europe, technological change had altered the American lifestyle. Industry flourished. Cities grew. Mechanization spread. It was an era of progress threatened only by distant fighting. Americans were enjoying the products of science and technology. It was natural that their government would turn to its scientific and industrial resources when it began to prepare for war.

Edison Plants a Seed

The Navy was first to react to the need to channel research toward military problems. In 1915, Secretary of the Navy Josephus Daniels appointed a Naval Consulting Board and asked Thomas A. Edison to be its chairman. Daniels had written to the great inventor:

. . .one of the imperative needs of the Navy. . .is machinery and facilities for utilizing the natural inventive genius of Americans to meet the new conditions of warfare as shown abroad. . .a department of invention and development, to which all ideas and suggestions, either from the service or from civilian inventors, can be referred for determination for us to take up and perfect.

The engineers and inventors who made up the board (there were few actual scientists) began to study a very wide range of scientific and technological problems in the physical sciences, engineering, munitions, communications, ship propulsion, navigation, and even personnel health and welfare. They were quick to realize that these problems could not be solved without adequate research facilities. So they proposed a naval laboratory under an officer's command with a staff of "civilian experimenters, chemists, physicists, etc.," where inventors could develop practical solutions to military problems. Daniels and a few members went before Congress with the Board's recommendations and received an appropriation of $1,000,000 for the laboratory.

Before any of the money was spent, the United States was at war and the National Research Council was directing the whole wartime research structure. The Naval Consulting Board began studying means to combat the submarine and screening the random variety of inventions that civilian tinkerers contributed to the war effort. Meanwhile, with its "dreadnaught" battleships leading the way, the U.S. Navy fought with a fleet built in peacetime by forward-thinking leaders who knew the value of science and technology.

The research establishment grew large and important during the war. Scientists in government, in universities, and in industry pooled their efforts to find immediate remedies for the problems of the new combat technology. New weapons begot new defenses. New development in communications, transportation, and medicine were exploited and studied further. Then the armistice came and the tools of research were put down along with the guns. The American people, tired of war, rejected everything connected with it. The scientific activity supported so fervently by the government while the fighting was going on had difficulty finding a peacetime role.

A Lab to Call Its Own

The Navy held one advantage againt this postwar decline of science: the Congressional authorization for the laboratory proposed by the Naval Consulting Board in 1916. After a few years of discussion among Navy planners as to what the laboratory should be, what it should do, and where it should be located, ground was broken for the first building in 1920 beside the Potomac River in Washington, D.C. The facility was dedicated and commissioned three years later, on July 2, 1923, as the U.S. Naval Experimental and Research Laboratory, becoming, as Assistant Secretary of the Navy Theodore

A crewmember stands watch in the Combat Information Center aboard the AEGIS cruiser *USS Bunker Hill*.

Roosevelt, Jr., called, "an instrument whereby Navy men are encouraged to work constantly for advancement in naval science." In other words, the laboratory gave the Navy, for the first time, a direct hand in performing scientific research in a facility established exclusively for that purpose.

Work began right away. A. Hoyt Taylor and Harvey C. Hayes led a group of civilian scientists from the Bureau of Engineering to form the staff of the new lab and continue experiments begun before the war on both radio and underwater sound detection. Their immediate purpose was to overcome the deficiencies the fleet had demonstrated during the war. Their long-range objective was to bring basic science into service for the Navy, to make more scientific knowledge available to solve future Navy problems. Although commanded by a regular

officer, the civilian scientists developed a strong *esprit* among themselves. Their pride was reflected in their work and justified by their achievements:

1923—Developed first high power, high frequency radio transmitter. Conducted first radio-controlled flight of a pilotless aircraft.

1924—Built first mobile transmitter and receiver and installed it aboard the airship *Shenandoah*.

1925—Developed electronic "pulse" transmitter (principle of radar).

1926—Formulated theory of "skip distance" effect of radio waves, the foundation of modern wave propagation theory.

1929—Demonstrated potentialities of VHF for naval communications.

1930—Developed new acoustic receiver for underwater sound detection, forerunner of modern echo-ranging sonar.

1933—Developed gamma-ray radiography which revolutionized inspection techniques used to detect flaws in cast and welded steels.

1934—Built and tested world's first pulse radar; developed first radar apparatus.

1938—Installed first operational radar on board ship. Devised IFF equipment for identifying friendly naval aircraft. Demonstrated radio systems for homing aircraft on carriers.

1939—Developed liquid thermal diffusion process for separating uranium isotopes and produced some of the material used in early atomic devices. Demonstrated potentialities of UHF for naval communications.

As scientists at the Naval Research Laboratory continued to make dramatic improvements in naval technology, the size of the facility grew along with its prestige. NRL stimulated interest in research among other Navy commands while it expanded its own programs to include radio and radar, acoustics, chemistry, physical optical metallurgy, thermodynamics, mechanics and electricity. Yet, even while the Navy relished its foresight in having created NRL and equipped its fleet with the revolutionary products of naval research, it became apparent that it could not keep pace with a war that demanded more than the Navy alone could provide. When the United States entered World War II, it was with the realization that the course of the war would be determined by weapons yet to be developed.

The second war in Europe generated another national mobilization of scientific resources. Applying lessons learned during World War I when he was Assistant secretary of the Navy, President Franklin Roosevelt created the National Defense Research Council in 1940, to direct the large pool of scientific talent to be focused on weapons research. A year later, the Office of Scientific Research and Development (OSRD) was established with the larger role "to assure maximum utilization of [scientific] personnel and resources in *developing* and *applying* the results of scientific research to defense purposes." (Emphasis added.) OSRD became the coordinator between independent research and that carried on within the Army and Navy.

Research activities were already well coordinated within the Navy, especially at NRL. Scientists there were making remarkable progress in developing and refining applications of their work, especially in communications, radar and sonar. They also continued to undertake new projects, as they did in 1939, when NRL became the first U.S. Government agency to study atomic power.

Elsewhere in the Navy, a growing number of scientists, engineers and technicians were engaged in a variety of experimental work geared to particular naval problems or capabilities. The Bureau of Ordnance, for example, was busily testing new developments in gunnery, munitions and bomb delivery. That bureau also operated the Naval Ordnance Laboratory which had been opened at the Washington Navy Yard in 1929 to pursue the field of naval mine development.

All this experimental work supported the larger, more visible improvements in the design and function for both ships and aircraft. The Navy was incorporating these improvements in an awesome new fleet of destroyers, battleships, submarines and aircraft carriers. Naval operations were becoming more specialized to counter the multiple threat from air, surface and undersea arenas. Specialists in hydrodynamic and aerodynamic engineering who tackled the problems created by these new technologies were the architects of the Navy's new look. They were aided by the establishment of the David Taylor Model Basin in 1939, at Carderock, Maryland, another new facility reflecting the Navy's increased reliance on scientific support of fleet operations. The wisdom of that reliance became apparent all too suddenly as the Navy was called upon first to protect the sea lanes former merchant ships bearing arms and supplies for European allies, then recover quickly from the Japanese attack on its own ships at Pearl Harbor.

Thus, were all the scientific resources of the United States put to work, military and civilian researchers united by the common urgency to get the job done. Essentially their task was to strengthen combat technology—develop new weapons and defense systems, put the new developments into operational use, and solve new problems encountered in military and naval actions—and to do it quickly. It was a circular process. The course of the war determined what scientific work was done; the results of the scientific work determined the course of the war.

Science did as much to determine the outcome of World War II as did politics or economics. It was also as much a contributor to the emergence of the United States

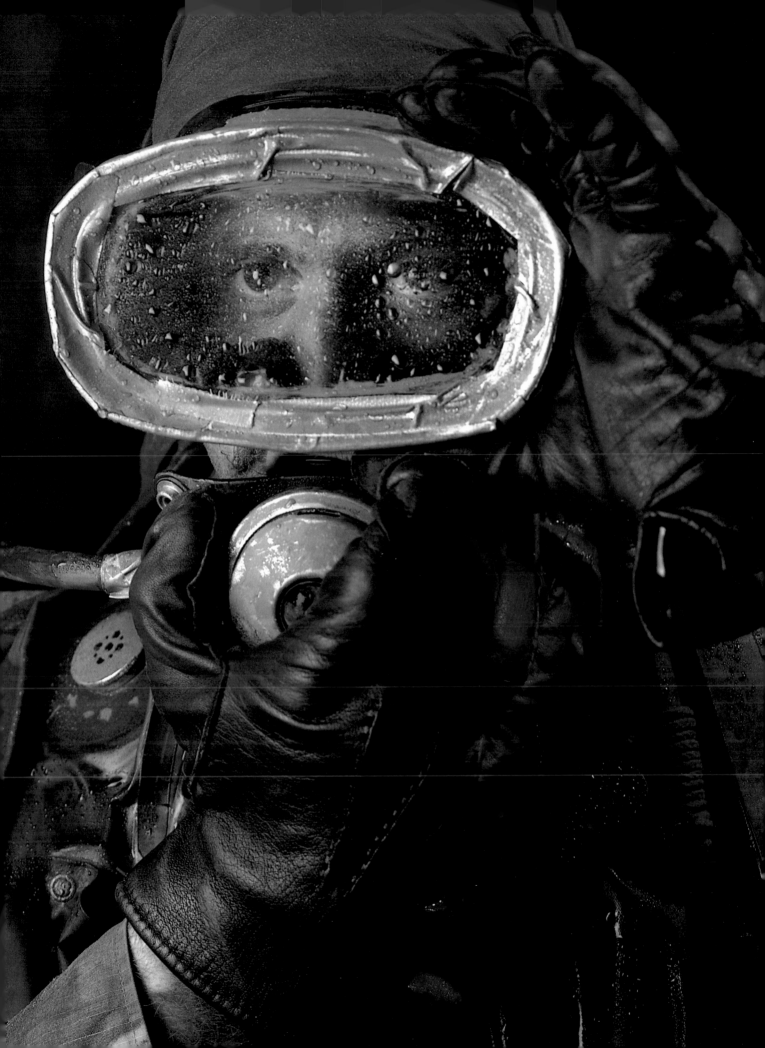

as a major world power. Indeed, the partnership of science and national defense had been so successful that many responsible people did not want that partnership dissolved by traditional postwar retrenchment. They wanted, instead, to translate the emergency, wartime dependence of government on science into the cooperative, peacetime interdependence of each.

A means to this end was suggested by Vannevar Bush, director of the Office of Scientific Research and Development, in his report of July 1945, "Science, the Endless Frontier." Bush's premise was that only the systematic pursuit of research on a broad front, with Federal support, would insure the choices the nation would need to pursue its objectives. The key word was "choices," according to the report, for science produces neither tools nor technology to solve national problems; it offers only options from which to choose the right course.

The Bush Report convinced Secretary of the Navy James Forrestal and some of his associates that science was a worthy investment for the Navy. They, in turn, convinced some members of Congress to introduce a bill to establish an office of naval research, an agency

patterned after the OSRD and some of Bush's suggestions. The bill became Public Law 79-588 when President Truman signed it, August 3, 1946. (The Law was actually approved by Congress on August 1, which is the date the Office of Naval Research celebrates its establishment.) It was the U.S. Government's first peacetime venture into large-scale support of basic science, and its charter was clearly stated:

To establish an Office of Naval Research in the Department of the Navy; to plan, foster, and encourage scientific research in recognition of its paramount importance as related to the maintenance of future naval power, and the preservation of national security; to provide within the Department of the Navy a single office, which, by contract and otherwise, shall be able to obtain, coordinate and make available to all bureaus and activities of the Department of the Navy, worldwide scientific information and the necessary services for conducting specialized and imaginative research; to establish a Naval Research Advisory Committee consisting of persons preeminent in the fields of science and research, to consult with and advise the Chief of such Office in matters pertaining to research.

The words of Public Law 588 were put into practice by a group of highly motivated naval officers and scientists who first staffed the Office of Naval Research—ONR. They molded the components of a few wartime research offices into a unique organization authorized to support the basic research of civilian scientists as well as to direct the work of the Navy's own researchers. Their most significant achievement was the creation of new contracting procedures which eliminated red tape in deference to the academic freedom necessary for good scientific inquiry. University scientists were allowed to do their chosen research under Navy sponsorship without Navy control.

The Navy chose to sponsor the scientists whose research was potentially useful to the Navy but the only control was in the choosing. The scientists' only obligations were to do the work they proposed and to share their findings with the Navy. It was an arrangement that pleased both the Navy and the scientists, because it gave both the opportunity for progress. For science, the new Navy research office provided new research opportunities; for the Navy,

ONR provided access to new knowledge which would, as Vannevar Bush suggested, increase the choices for developing new technology. Thus, the Navy became a patron, not merely a consumer, of science and its services.

In effect, ONR formed a bridge between civilian science and naval technology and the connection was mutually advantageous. By using science to stimulate naval technology with new knowledge, ONR was stimulating science with new research opportunities.

As coordinator of the Navy's widespread research interests, ONR has been successful translating new scientific knowledge into solutions of practical military value for the Navy. Under ONR's guidance, basic research in a variety of fields, from astronomy to zoology, has been used to improve every facet of naval technology.

New designs and systems for surface ships and submarines, the Polaris missile and now the Trident, high performance aircraft, navigation and communication satellites, solid-state electronics for data processing, communications, radar and sonar, systems for underwater survival and exploration (such as the bathyscaphe *Trieste* which, in 1960, dove seven miles

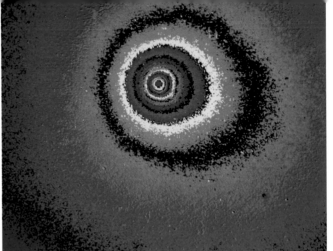

A graduate student works in the physiology lab at the Uniformed Services University of the Health Sciences.

An ultraviolet image of Comet Halley, taken by Navy scientists; a damage control exercise aboard *USS Bunker Hill.*

down to the abysses of the ocean, and *Argo-Jason* used in 1985 and 1986 to discover and explore the sunken passenger liner *Titanic,* were all made possible by research supported by the Office of Naval Research.

ONR literally helped to launch an era of tremendous scientific achievement, which has played an important role in strengthening our entire national defense structure. One can readily recognize that the strength of today's Navy reflects the Navy's tradition of scientific achievement, a tradition that has been carried by ONR for over 40 years.

Since 1980, ONR has been closely joined in scientific and technological efforts by the Office of Naval Technology (ONT). ONT was established to provide a more clearly defined process for the planning and execution of programs within the Navy's technology arena and transition of these programs into high stages of development. The Office eventually became a component of the Chief of Naval Research in 1985. While ONR is concerned with investigating science opportunities at the basic level, ONT's principal efforts

are directed toward development of technology for application to Navy and Marine Corps mission areas. These areas include antiaircraft, antiship, and antisubmarine warfare systems; nuclear propulsion; surveillance; command, control and communications; and technologies associated with every facet of ship, submarine and aircraft systems. In other words, what ONR generally begins, ONT spurs on to reality.

Defense technologies conceived and carried forward through naval research include the maser and the laser, the electronically suspended gyroscope, and modern electronic navigation systems. Navy research funding supported the first man-in-the-sea efforts which established the physiological limits to man's ability to live and work in the ocean's depth. The first true deep-diving submersible, *Alvin,* constructed for the Navy, opened most of the ocean bottom to manned exploration and provided a critical tool for search and recovery. In July 1986, *Alvin,* and a remote vehicle called "*J.J.,*" explored the wreck of the passenger liner, *Titanic,* discovered nearly a year earlier by deep ocean search equipment designed for the Navy. Scientists using *Alvin* also located underwater volcanic fields and discovered deep sea life forms unknown to exist before. Another Navy first among many thousand.

The Navy conducts marine mammal research with Weddell seals in Antarctica.

The full value of Navy research efforts cannot be measured by what it has done for the Navy alone. The basic and advanced research that allowed the Navy to improve its fleet has given the civilian domain the same advanced technology, finding its way into businesses, hospitals, homes and schools.

By-products of naval research can be found on the job. Navy studies in human engineering have helped to improve the designs of industrial equipment and machinery by analyzing the design of the human beings who operate them. Blending man and machine in these ways results in greater safety, greater efficiency and greater productivity. The machines themselves have been made more reliable with the help of better lubricants and strong metal alloys developed by naval research. In a less tangible way, Navy research in group psychology has been providing important information on how people perform in an organizational setting. Such information is valuable to both management and labor.

Every organization has been affected by computer technology. It is interesting to note that the world's first high-speed digital computer was developed by scientists supported by ONR. Naval research has also contributed to better health care. The best example is the invention and refinement of a method for freezing blood for long term storage. Unfrozen blood may be stored for a maximum of 21 days, but the new method of freezing permits storage for up to 10 years. The technique is especially valuable for preserving rare blood types for use in emergency situations. Blood donated today may save a life several years from now. ONR continues to fund research for improving long-term storage of blood and developing a universal blood type which can be used in blood transfusions regardless of the blood type of the recipient.

The exciting new science of bionics—designing machines to duplicate biological functions—has received a lot of Navy attention. Many people think of robots when bionics is mentioned, but it involves much more, especially where medical technology is concerned. One naval laboratory developed a super-sensitive instrument that diagnoses vision defects by measuring optical impulses, or brain waves. Using this instrument, a doctor can examine someone's eyes without having to rely on the patients' description of what he or she sees. The technique has already proved useful in the treatment of visual disorders in infants and small children. Navy studies in bionics have also helped to improve the designs of artificial limbs. For example, a motor-driven mechanical arm can be entirely controlled by an individual's shoulder muscles.

Another medical application of Navy-sponsored research that has been developed recently is a method of healing bone fractures more quickly by applying a small electric current to the fracture. The Navy is also actively participating in biomedical research on human and animal diseases.

The most visible examples of the use of naval research can be found in and around our homes. Modern packaging material, such as sandwich wrapping, resulted from research by the Navy to make strong, thin, plastic balloons to study the upper atmosphere. Naval research also provided much of the basic knowledge used to develop many other new materials, including fiberglass, Teflon, stronger adhesives and plastics. The development of the transistor and all the related marvels of the electronics industry are the products of basic research in solid-state physics supported, on a large scale, by the Navy. Navy research also led to the design of the lithium dry cell battery that is several times more powerful and more durable than conventional dry cells. Unlike ordinary batteries, it will not lose its power when not in use. It delivers full power no matter how long it remains idle. The Marine Corps considers the battery exceptionally useful as a power source for portable communications equipment. The battery can also be used to power emergency lighting systems and fire alarms.

Other Navy-oriented projects funded by the Navy which have produced results which can, and have had application in the civilian community, include: methods of clearing fog from airports, resulting from investigations in atmospheric science; a long-term research effort in fluid lubrication and gas bearings that produced the gyroscopes now used in inertial navigation systems. These same gas bearings are common now in high speed tape transport and in flying heads for computer disk memory.

Other civilian spin-offs of Navy research include new metals and alloys; stronger, lighter and corrosion proof composite materials; paints and lubricants, and a host of other products and techniques used in the home, industry and institutions.

Perhaps the largest impact of naval research has been felt in our schools. Navy efforts to improve the quality of its training programs have helped to make new methods and equipment available to civilian education. The continuing support of university scientists, under the concept pioneered by ONR, has allowed academic institutions to add whole new chapters to our science textbooks. The tremendous fund of knowledge generated by this research has had a profound effect on education itself. No one can deny that students today are learning a great deal more about science at earlier ages than their parents did 20 or 30 years ago.

Recent Navy programs which support the enhancement of science and technology within the academic community of our nation include the Young Investigators Program. The YIP program, as it is known, is intended to attract the best young academic researchers on a tenure track at U.S. universities to areas of research that are important to the Navy's future requirements.

Another enhancement are the four research chairs in oceanography which Secretary of the Navy John F. Lehman, Jr., instituted in 1985. The objective of these chairs is to ensure a strong Navy ocean science program by attracting the best academic scientists and students to work on oceanography. In addition, Secretary Lehman directed the creation of the Institute for Naval Oceanography for conducting ocean modeling efforts for research and development programs leading to better and in many cases new capabilities for ocean forecasting.

The Navy has been supporting programs to encourage students to pursue higher education in engineering and science for several years, because maintaining a cadre of well-trained young scientists is vital to the future of naval science and to the future of our nation. Among these programs are:

- The ONR Fellowship Program, which awards each year 40 three-year fellowships to outstanding graduates to pursue work for a doctoral degree in areas of science and engineering critical to the Navy.
- The Apprentice Program, which provides a platform from which ONR investigators can hire high school students during the summer to assist on research projects, and encourage careers in science and engineering.
- The Naval Science Awards Program, which provides up to $10,000 college scholarships, science-oriented trips in the U.S. and abroad for those high school students who excel in state, regional, Navy national and international science fair and project competitions. Here, again, the purpose is to encourage careers in science and engineering.

The contributions of naval research and support go far beyond these few examples mentioned. In more

Midshipmen at the U.S. Naval Academy practice marching on the parade field.

recent years, new vistas of our world's oceans were captured on film for the first time by a Navy astronaut, oceanographer Paul Scully-Power. Similarly, Dr. John-David Bartoe, a physicist at the Naval Research Laboratory, went aloft in a shuttle flight to study solar phenomena. Yet another physicist, Dr. Jerome Karle, also employed at NRL, and a fellow scientist who formerly worked at NRL, won the Nobel prize for chemistry in 1985, for research in crystal development, exemplifying that good science can be performed by dedicated government scientists.

The world leadership of the United States in basic research in the four decades following World War II has been attributed in great part to the timely and imaginative work of Navy-sponsored eminent scientists. About half of all Nobel laureates in the physical sciences at one time or other worked on projects funded by the

Office of Naval Research. Dr. Karle is the Navy's first employee-laurate.

Like the rest of society, the Navy is deeply concerned about contemporary problems—the economy, the environment and the enigma of human behavior. Current naval research is addressing these problems directly and indirectly, in a variety of programs. For example, the Navy is participating in studies concerning the effectiveness of job training programs, human factors in mining and manufacturing operations, pollution control and how to eliminate pollution, energy alternatives to fossil fuels, weather prediction and control of the weather, human and animal behavior, and the extensive exploration of the deep ocean and development of its abundant food and mineral resources.

These and the many other research programs conducted or supported by the Navy are actively creating opportunities to solve the global problems that

Retrieving their hats is the last thing on the minds of these Naval Academy graduates.

face us. The problems are complex and they will not change for the better overnight. In response to this, the Navy believes in continuing to steadily work for change, instead of waiting for change to just happen.

Prospect and Retrospect

The growth and accomplishment of ONR, during the last 40 years, and ONT, during the past seven years, make up the current chapter of the Navy's 212 years of experience with science. It can be noted, that the last four decades of naval research coincide with a period of tremendous scientific achievement in the United States, an era variously called "the nuclear age," "the computer age," or "the space age." The technological advances these names express are the products of research fostered in part by the Navy in its efforts to maintain a fleet that *"reflects the highest scientific resource of its day."*

That philosophy, articulated by Secretary Whitney in 1885, is one under which the Navy has operated, to varying degrees, since David Bushnell was summoned to demonstrate his Turtle in 1776. It was that philosophy which led President Washington to accept Joshua Humphrey's frigate designs. It governed the thinking of men like John Quincy Adams, Charles Wilkes, and Matthew Fontain Maury, whose collective efforts enhanced the value of science and enlarged the Navy's role in the use of it. It fashioned the change from wooden sailing ships to steamers and ironclads to steel battleships, guided missile cruisers and nuclear powered aircraft carriers. It endured postwar retrenchments to develop the submarine and the airplane. It created laboratories and other resources to revolutionize the fleet. That philosophy strengthens the affinity between the Navy and science and, as this examination of history has revealed, it weaves the pattern of a proud naval tradition that continues to the present day. ⌐⊤

Now Hear This

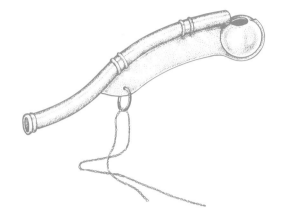

THE NEXT TIME you hear a boatswain's pipe signaling an impending call for all hands to quarters for muster, just think that this "music" has been heard by sailors of our Navy for the last 212 years. It may not be beautiful music—but take note that you'll be listening to the most ancient and distinctive nautical sound effect of them all. In fact, the oarsmen on ancient Greek and Roman galleys are said to have timed their strokes either to a pipe or flute. And during the days of the Crusades, a pipe was employed (in the English Navy) as a signal for the crossbowmen to come up on deck for an attack.

The present form of the boatswain's instrument (properly termed a "call") was established some time during the 16th century. After defeating Scotland's Andrew Barton, England's Lord Howard took a pipe from the fallen body of his foe, and when he became Lord High Admiral, he officially adopted it. In time it came to be used for passing of orders as well as salutes to distinguished visitors—as it is today.

In the days of sail there were certain very definite and practical uses for the pipes, some of which have passed into history. Men high on the royal and t'gallant yards, for example, could hear its piercing call rising from the deck above the howl of the winds. In those days of sail, merchant as well as naval vessels carried piping boatswain's mates, but the pipe has long since ceased to be a feature of anything but a man-of-war.

Let's clarify a couple of terms before we go any further. We said earlier that the instrument itself is properly, a "call." However, the various "words" which were passed by the call are also known as calls. So, to avoid confusion, and at the risk of offending purists, the instrument will be called hereafter by its popular misnomer—the boatswain's pipe.

Here, culled from the files of the Navy's popular news and feature magazine, "All Hands," are some interesting items about the boatswain's pipe—including some tips on how to play a call yourself.

Chances are if you've ever served or visited aboard a Navy ship for any length of time—say 24 hours or so—you've probably already heard a medley of sounds destined to become among the most familiar of your Navy career. As a matter of fact, there have no doubt been occasions when you've harbored a barely suppressed desire to tell "that guy up on the quarterdeck what he could do with his licorice stick."

If you're like most of us, while you've got a pretty good idea of the "why for" and the "when," you're probably not too clear on the "how's it done."

Read on, if you will. A more thorough knowledge of the procedures involved in sounding a boatswain's pipe is bound to increase your "musical appreciation" when next you hear those dulcet tones. And who knows—you might be inspired to master the art yourself. You wouldn't be the first. Plenty of Navy men and women—mostly deck or ordnance ratings, to be sure, such as gunner's mates, torpedomen and quartermasters, but more than one yeoman, radioman and what have you—have done just that, and take pride in their ability to handle the pipe as well as any boatswain's mate around.

Let's start off with a definite premise—that there's much more involved in piping a call properly than simply picking up a pipe and applying lung power at the correct end.

To begin with, all of the distinct and different sounds

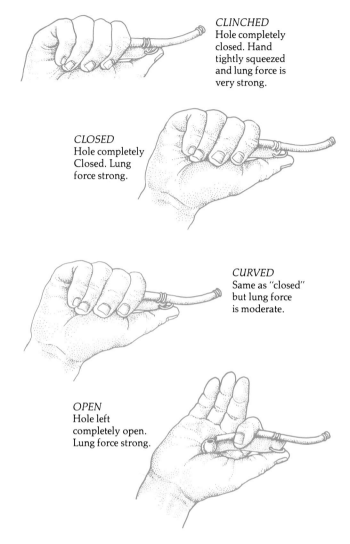

CLINCHED
Hole completely closed. Hand tightly squeezed and lung force is very strong.

CLOSED
Hole completely Closed. Lung force strong.

CURVED
Same as "closed" but lung force is moderate.

OPEN
Hole left completely open. Lung force strong.

are achieved through, and affected by, several methods of cupping the pipe in the hand. More on this later.

Then there's the pipe itself—a more complicated affair than you might imagine. The ship's First Lieutenant is provided with an original issue of pipes, which usually don't last very long. Boatswain's mates, it seems, have a habit when being transferred of packing off with their pipes still attached to their persons. Most of them, however, eventually prefer to buy their own particular model, oftentimes with an ornamental design worked around it.

G.I. or tailor-made, though, a pipe won't sound worth listening to until it's tuned. Pipes are stamped out when manufactured, and both the hole in the top of the bowl and the aperture in the reed next to it (the pee) are nearly always misshapen. The pee must be cut off clean at an angle, then the hole filed down until the blast of air from the pee is exactly split by the hole's outer edge. A nail file is ideal for this operation, you'll find. It has a fine grain, and is thin enough to file down the bowl without also cutting the pee.

Once this considerable filing down of the bowl is accomplished, a straw shoved through the reed should split on the far edge of the hole. When this occurs, the pipe is about right. Occasionally, however, there may be a gap between the bottom of the pee and the bowl. This will cause a hissing sound of escaping air which will interfere with the clearness of the call. A drop of solder in the gap will remedy that condition.

We mentioned before that there was more to sounding the boatswain's pipe than might at first glance seem apparent. The various calls, for example have been reduced to paper, somewhat in the fashion of musical scores. Now these "scores" are fairly simple and easy to figure out (if you could find a copy of the Bluejacket's Manual). But remember those different hand positions we referred to a while back?

It would be a complete waste of time, for instance, to attempt to sound a sustained note with the pipe held in either the curved or closed position. Those are used exclusively as starting or stopping positions, or as an intermediate step in rising from the open to the clinched position. Then too, just about the toughest part for a beginner, we're told, is learning to sound the high, shrill scream which issues forth when the pipe is properly held in the clinched position. To achieve this you must squeeze hard and blow hard.

An added thought—you might be wise to stage your first practice session down in the bilges of your own boat, away on vacation in the wilderness, or at least out of earshot of family or shipmates.

At first you probably won't produce much but a noise resembling the sound of escaping steam, but don't let that discourage you. Before long you'll be "piping up" as well as the saltiest boatswain's mate. At least you'll think so.

Where can you buy one? Join the Navy or make friends with an active duty or retired Navy man or woman. Or check the ship's store associated with the United States Navy Memorial.

One final bit of advice. If you want to live until tomorrow, NEVER practice "piping" in a car or other small, closed space. And if you have a big brother or sister, don't "pipe" reveille next to his or her bed in the morning. ⌁

An Old Salt's Old Salt

Millie Tamberg

Problems?

Everyone has their share, but most people don't try to take on someone else's—except for Thomas C. Oneyear.

Why?

Because that's his job.

As command master chief for Assault Craft Unit (ACU) Two at Little Creek Naval Amphibious Base in Norfolk, Virginia, Oneyear helps solve day-to-day problems for the more than 300 men and women assigned to the unit.

"I'm the waterfront supervisor for all the craftmasters and coxswains (men in charge of small craft)," says the boatswain's mate.

Although Oneyear is assigned to shore duty, he works amid a fleet of mechanized landing craft (LCMs or Mike-eights) and utility landing craft (LCUs). The 74-foot-long Mike-eights and the 134-foot-long LCUs support the unit's dual mission of transporting troops and equipment to and from amphibious assaults and training boat crews.

Because these crews operate at sea and on the beach, they are known as the amphibious Navy and dubbed "Gators."

"Gators are a unique part of the Navy," says Oneyear. "We're not fancy cruiser or battleship sailors—like I used to be—but we get an important job done. If you look back in history you'll read about the operations they've done--D-Day and Iwo Jima, for example—and you'll find that the unsung heroes were the boat coxswains."

Those assigned to the Norfolk-based unit who deploy to the Atlantic, Mediterranean and Caribbean coasts to conduct periodic amphibious exercises often return to Norfolk with their own brand of problems for their command master chief.

"Sometimes when the crews come back from a deployment they come to me because they're not being paid correctly for their living quarters or food. I also deal with the average problems that other command master chiefs do, and those are marital problems and money management problems," he explains. "I deal with everything a sailor can get into while he's a young person maturing.

I'm also the command master chief—the senior enlisted advisor and direct liaison between the commanding officer and all the enlisted personnel at this command. In other words, I take care of all their problems."

What are the prerequisites for the job?

There was no formal schooling, according to Oneyear, just the combination of assignments and working with people throughout his Navy career.

"I've been to the 'school of hard knocks'—25 years in the Navy, 12 ships, two tours in Vietnam, and two tours of 'pushing boots,' " says the former recruit company commander in a raspy baritone voice.

"I've commissioned the USS Dubuque (an amphibious transport ship), Yellowstone and Shenandoah (destroyer tenders), and recommissioned the battleship Iowa," boasts the Dubuque, Iowa, native. "I've decommissioned a few too."

Oneyear's well-rounded career is evidenced by three different breast insignia indicating special qualifications, and a colorful array of ribbons—some awarded two and three times. And nautical tattoos on the fingers of both hands, wrists and ear lobes, not to mention the gold

Millie Tamberg is a Navy journalist assigned to the Navy Public Affairs Center in Norfolk, Virginia

inlayed crossed anchors in two front teeth—each holding a sea story of its own—are outdone only by those his uniform covers.

Besides two tours in Vietnam, the 42-year-old sea service veteran has made two around-the-world cruises, nine to the Caribbean, eight to the Western Pacific, seven to the Mediterranean and five to the North Atlantic.

Because Oneyear is a husband and father of two, he appreciates the types of problems Navy men and women with families face, and takes a different approach with their problems.

"We have an Ombudsman (wife of a unit member who assists other wives with their problems) for our command who is a very young lady, but if I have someone who is a little older and needs to talk to someone with a little more experience, then I'll let them talk with 'ma'—my wife Cheryl," he says. "It's just a nice touch, and it does work. The job can get nerve-racking at times, but the satisfaction comes with knowing that people are being taken care of."

Focusing on Naval History

FROM TALL SHIPS to submarines, biplanes to nuclear-powered aircraft carriers—the United States Navy has evolved. Although the complexity and technological development of our nation's ships, aircraft and weapons systems have changed steadily throughout history, the dedication, resolve, commitment, loyalty and ingenuity of Navy men and women have remained constant. In more than 210 years, our Navy has accomplished too many things for inclusion in this book, but at least some of the more notable and significant events deserve special attention here.

12 JUN 1775
First engagement at sea during the Revolution. Citizens of Machias, Maine, under the command of Jeremiah O'Brien, seized a cargo sloop taking lumber to Boston and with it captured the cutter *HM Margaretta*.

06 SEP 1775
The schooner *Hannah* sails as first unit of George Washington's Navy of converted merchantmen. Seven others followed suit: *Lynch, Franklin, Lee, Harrison, Warren, Washington* and *Hancock*

A Navy is Born

13 OCT 1775
The Second Continental Congress met at Philadelphia, approving the acquisition and fitting out of two naval vessels: the 24-gun ship *Alfred* and the 20-gun ship *Columbus*. Within three months, our Navy grew to include the brigs *Andrea Doria* and *Cabot*; two sloops, *Providence* and *Hornet* and two schooners, *Wasp* and *Fly*.

14 FEB 1778
John Paul Jones sailed into Quiberon Bay, France, aboard *Ranger*, and received the first official recognition by a foreign power of the American "Stars and Stripes" flag—a nine-gun salute. (Lieutenant John Paul Jones hoisted the first official American flag on a ship, *Alfred*, on 03 December 1775. And on 16 November 1776 that flag was saluted by the Dutch Governor of St. Eustatius Island in the West Indies.)

24 APR 1778
John Paul Jones, in command of the sloop *Ranger*, defeated the sloop *HMS Drake* off Belfast, Ireland. *Drake* became the first major British warship to be taken by the New Navy.

23 SEP 1779
John Paul Jones was again the main character during a notable event and the author of a statement that was symbolic of the spirit of the newborn Navy. Aboard *Bonhomme Richard*, Jones and his crew defeated the superior British frigate *Serapis*. The highlight of the battle came when, after being asked if he had struck colors, Jones replied, "Struck, sir? I have not yet begun to fight!"

U.S. Navy—The Early Years

Between America's two wars with Great Britain, the early U.S. Navy was involved in two other conflicts. The first was the "Quasi-War" with France, 1798-1801, which was entirely a naval war. It followed worsening diplomatic relations with France, including a refusal by the French secretary of foreign affairs, Talleyrand, to receive U.S. representatives unless a bribe was paid and a loan granted. The famous expression "Millions for defense, but not one cent for tribute," originated at this time. The Quasi-War was the baptism of fire for the United States Navy under the new Constitution. Such historic ships as *USS Constellation, Constitution* and *United States* were in this action.

16 FEB 1804

In response to the Barbary States that were forcing other nations to pay ransom for safe passage through the Mediterranean Sea, Lieutenant Stephen Decatur and 84 seamen slipped into the harbor at Tripoli and burned the captured frigate *Philadelphia*. Not a single Navy man was lost, and Britain's Admiral Lord Nelson described the raid as "one of the most bold and daring acts of the age."

The War of 1812

Brought on in part by British impressment of American seamen, the War of 1812 soon became an excuse for England to make her presence felt and demonstrate her power on the American continent.

19 AUG 1812

Captain Isaac Hull in *Constitution* defeated the British frigate *Guerriere. Constitution* earned her nickname "*Old Ironsides*" here, and the victory convinced the Congress and President Madison of the need for a strong Navy to protect and defend the country.

10 SEP 1813

Captain Oliver Hazard Perry defeated a British squadron on Lake Erie and sent his dispatch, "We have met the enemy and they are ours." Perry's victory gained control of Lake Erie and strengthened the American claim to the Northwest Territory.

Important Strides

23 APR 1814

USS Robert Fulton, the world's first fully steam-powered warship was launched in New York City. Originally called *Demologos*, it was renamed for the inventor who worked on its design and construction.

Continental Navy sloop *Alfred*, flagship of Lieutenant John Paul Jones, raised the Grand Union flag while at anchor in Phladelphia on December 3, 1775; right, burning of the frigate *Philadelphia* in the harbor of Tripoli on February 16, 1804.

17 JAN 1840
Lieutenant Charles Wilkes visited the subpolar region in an Antarctic exploration which proved conclusively that the icy land was a continent.

05 SEP 1843
USS Princeton, the Navy's first successful propeller-driven steamship was launched. She had an innovative propeller which eliminated the vulnerable paddlewheels and permitted the ship's engines to be placed in protected, below-deck spaces.

27 MAR 1846
The Mexican War gave birth to a model for amphibious warfare that was to last a hundred years. It called for landing 10,000 U.S. troops at Vera Cruz, said to be one of the most powerful fortresses in the Western Hemisphere. Marines marched with Scott into Mexico City on 14 Sep from whence came the phrase "halls of Montezuma" in the famed Marines' song.

31 MAR 1854
Commodore Matthew C. Perry signed a treaty with Japan which opened their ports to American trade and provisioning of ships. England and Russia followed with their own treaties modeled after Perry's.

Commodore Perry establishes trade with Japan.

9 MAR 1862
A tight Union Blockade of the South led to this first ironclad battle, fought between *USS Monitor* and *CSS Virginia* (ex *USS Merrimack*) at Hampton Roads,

USS Merrimack at Hampton Roads, Virginia.

Virginia. After four hours, *Virginia* broke off the engagement and no one could say who won, but it did prevent the blockade from being broken. The battle ensured Union supremacy at sea and made wooden Navy ships obsolete. (Except for mine sweepers in the next century)

17 FEB 1864
CSS H. L. Hunley conducted first successful submarine attack when she torpedoed and sank the steam sloop of war *USS Housatonic* at Charleston, South Carolina.

05 AUG 1864
Admiral David G. Farragut damned the torpedoes and went full speed ahead to win the Battle of Mobile Bay. This victory closed the South's most important port (since New Orleans had already fallen) and tightened the Union blockade. Along with Sherman's capture of Atlanta, Farragut's victory may have been one of the factors leading to the reelection of President Abraham Lincoln.

Spanish-American War

15 FEB 1898
A terrific explosion tore through the hull of the battleship *USS Maine* while at anchor in Havana Harbor, killing 250 American Navymen. The real cause of the explosion has never been uncovered, but it was a factor leading to the Spanish-American War. "Remember the Maine" became our battle cry.

01 May 1898
Commodore George Dewey sailed into Manila Bay and ordered, "You may fire when you are ready, Gridley." Dewey's resounding victory destroyed Spain's naval power in the East and was instrumental in bringing the war to a swift conclusion.

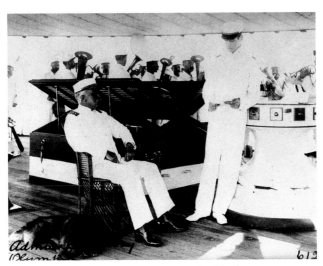
Admiral George Dewey aboard *USS Olympia.*

03 Jul 1898
U.S. naval forces at Cuba cornered the Spanish Atlantic Squadron at Santiago Bay, and as the Spanish ships tried to break out of the bay, they were demolished. Cuba and Puerto Rico fell shortly afterwards.

Turn of the Century

12 Apr 1900
The Navy accepts its first operational submarine, *USS Holland*, a cigar-shaped craft, 52 feet long and 10 feet in diameter.

16 Dec 1907
The Great White Fleet departed Hampton Roads, Virginia, for an around the world cruise, demonstrating U.S. power and resolve and successfully thwarting a developing war with Japan over the Open Door Policy.

06 Apr 1909
Navy's involvement in exploration continued during the century's first decade: Commander Robert E. Peary, accompanied by Matthew Henson, achieved the long-sought goal of reaching the North Pole.

14 Nov 1910
Despite wind and rain, Eugene Ely, in a Curtiss biplane, made the first takeoff from a ship. The flight was made from a wooden platform built on the bow of the cruiser *USS Birmingham* which was at anchor at Hampton Roads, Virginia. Ely landed safely on Willoughby Spit about two miles away. Less than a year later, his short flying career came to an end when he died in a crash.

18 Jan 1911
Eugene Ely rolled up the deck on *USS Pennsylvania* in a Curtiss pusher, in the world's first aircraft landing aboard a ship.

12 Apr 1911
Lieutenants Glenn Ellyson and Jack Towers began flight training under Glenn Curtiss, becoming the Navy's first aviators.

09 Sep 1911
The Navy launches its first destroyers—500-ton ships capable of 28 knots, they introduced improved fire control methods and telegraphy to the fleet.

Lieutenant David Ingalls, the Navy's only ace during World War I.

Anchors Aweigh

Lively march tempo

Stand Navy out sea, Fight our battle cry;
We'll never change our course, So vicious foe steer shy-y-y-y
Roll out the T.N.T. Anchors Aweigh—
Sail on to victory And skin their bones to Davy Jones, hooray!

Anchors Aweigh my boys, Anchors Aweigh—
Farewell to college joys, We'll sail at break of day-day-day-day!
Through our last night on shore, Drink to the foam,
Until we meet once more Here's wishing you a happy voyage home!

Words by CAPT Alfred H. Miles, USN (1907)
Revised lyrics by George D. Lottman
Music by LT Charles A. Zimmerman, USN

122

World War One

04 May 1917
Six American destroyers commanded by Commander Joseph K. Taussig steamed into Queenstown, Ireland, becoming the first U.S. Navy ships to commence operations in European waters. The event, billed as the "return of the *Mayflower*," was a great morale booster. The incident is probably best remembered by CDR Taussig's simple remark upon reporting to the British admiral in charge: "I shall be ready when refueled, sir."

17 Nov 1917
Destroyers *USS Nicholson* and *USS Fanning* were the first U.S. ships to sink an enemy submarine—U-58, 10 miles east of Queenstown, Ireland.

17 Sep-24 Nov 1917
Lieutenant Junior Grade David S. Ingalls, flying a Sopwith Camel over Nieuport, shot down his fifth enemy aircraft in six weeks, becoming the Navy's first ace . . . and the only one in World War I

The U.S. Navy's most significant World War I contribution was transporting and escorting millions of troops through submarine-infested waters without a loss in transit to Europe. In this effort, Navy destroyers played a vital role.

Between the Wars

27 May 1919
Navy flying boat NC-4 landed at Lisbon, Portugal, and became the first plane to complete a transatlantic flight. Continuing on to Portsmouth, England, her entire trip took less than 71 hours of flight time.

20 Mar 1922
The rebuilt collier, *Jupiter*, was commissioned *USS Langley*, and became the Navy's first aircraft carrier. On 17 October, the first landing while underway was accomplished by Lieutenant Commander G. deC. Chevalier.

May-Nov 1926
Lieutenant Commander Richard E. Byrd and Aviation Pilot Floyd Bennett made the first flight over the North Pole, in a Fokker trimotor named Josephine Ford, in May 1926. Six months later, Byrd flew the Ford trimotor Floyd Bennett over the South Pole, becoming the first man to fly over both poles.

The Navy's uniforms have changed dramatically from these worn by Yeomen during World War I, upper right; Commander Richard E. Byrd, dressed in furs, with his dog, Igloo, outside a hut during his Antarctic Expedition, April 1930.

World War Two

07 Dec 1941
Fifteen Navy ships were sunk or damaged, including all eight of the Pacific Fleet's battleships, when the Japanese bombed Pearl Harbor. Some 3,400 Navy and Marine Corps personnel were killed or wounded; the United States declared war on Japan the next day.

18 Apr 1942
Sixteen Army Air Force B-25s, commanded by Lieutenant Colonel "Jimmy" Doolittle, were launched from the aircraft carrier *USS Hornet* for an attack on Tokyo.

7-8 May 1942
The Battle of the Coral Sea was fought. The American victory stopped the Japanese advance toward Australia and New Zealand. It was the first battle in history where opposing ships did not exchange shots, but attacked each other with aircraft.

3-6 Jun 1942
Considered one of the most decisive battles in world history, the United States Navy defeated a Japanese invasion fleet heading for Midway Island. It altered the balance of power in the Pacific in favor of the Americans.

7 Aug 1942
The Marines landed on Guadalcanal. Last Japanese were not repelled until 09 February 1943.

06 Jun 1944
The Navy's most notable action in the Atlantic may have been its part in the Normandy Invasion, the largest amphibious operation in history. The greatest armada ever assembled carried out minesweeping, shore bombardment, amphibious operations and supply and troop transport. These enabled the Allies to successfully complete D-Day landings and eventually push on to Germany.

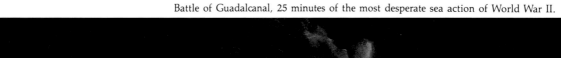

Battle of Guadalcanal, 25 minutes of the most desperate sea action of World War II.

Japanese surrender aboard *USS Missouri* in Tokyo Bay.

19 Jun 1944
The Battle of the Philippine Sea ended with the Japanese carrier forces short of ships, planes, gas and pilots. Unable to replace these, the Imperial Navy was never able to recover from her losses, although many desperate battles were to follow.

23 Oct 1944
In a last chance effort to salvage the Philippines, the Japanese sent a naval force to Leyte Gulf to attack the U.S. fleet. Their plan backfired and resulted in the deciding catastrophe for their Navy. With losses at Okinawa and Iwo Jima, the war in the Pacific was approaching its final days.

06 Aug 1945
The first atomic bomb was detonated over Hiroshima, Japan. Three days later, the second atomic bomb was dropped on Nagasaki, Japan.

02 Sep 1945
Japan formally surrendered on board the battleship *USS Missouri* at anchor in Tokyo Bay, Japan.

Korea

29 Jun 1950
Three days after the decision, supported by the United Nations, was made to give air and naval assistance to the Republic of Korea, the cruisers *USS Juneau* and *USS Dehaven* fired the first bombardment of the war.

15 Sep 1950
Most notable event of the war was the amphibious landing at Inchon, supported by massive shore bombardment by U.S. naval ships. This successful operation cut enemy communications, divided their forces and resistence dissolved. *USS Missouri's* shelling of supply roads far inland demonstrated a new concept of the Navy's ability to intervene in a ground operation whose main action is far inland.

From Korea to the Space Age

17 Jan 1955
USS Nautilus, the Navy's first atomic submarine, departed Long Island Sound on her maiden voyage.

31 Oct 1956
Que Sera Sera, a Navy R4D aircraft, became the first plane to land at the geographic South Pole. A seven-man party remained at the pole for 49 minutes and set up navigation aids for future flights.

Space Age

17 Mar 1958
Vanguard, a three-and-one-half-pound payload, developed by the Naval Research Laboratory, was placed into orbit to test the system designed for launching earth satellites during the International Geophysical Year.

03 Aug 1958
USS Nautilus became the first ship to reach the North Pole, as she passed under it on her way from Hawaii to the Atlantic.

09 Jun 1959
USS George Washington, our Navy's first nuclear ballistic missile submarine, was launched.

01 May 1960
A U-2 reconnaissance plane from the United States was shot down over the Soviet Union, leading to cancellation of an imminent Paris summit conference.

10 May 1960
The nuclear powered submarine *USS Triton* surfaced off the coast of Delaware after traveling 36,000 miles completely submerged. Her circumnavigation of the globe had taken 83 days and 10 hours.

15 Apr 1961
The nuclear powered, guided missile cruiser *USS Bainbridge* was launched.

17 Apr 1961
Invasion of Cuba's Bay of Pigs by Cuban exiles—trained, armed and directed by the U.S.—attempting to overthrow the regime of Premier Fidel Castro, was repulsed.

05 May 1961
Commander Alan B. Shepard, Jr. was rocketed from Cape Canaveral, Florida, 116.5 miles above the earth in a Mercury capsule, in the first U.S. manned sub-orbital space flight. The flight lasted 15 minutes.

09 Sep 1961
The nuclear- powered, guided missile cruiser *USS Long Beach* was commissioned.

25 Nov 1961
USS Enterprise, the Navy's first nuclear-powered aircraft carrier, was commissioned.

20 Feb 1962
Lt. Col. John H. Glenn, Jr., became the first American in orbit when he circled the earth three times in the Mercury capsule, "Friendship."

22 Oct 1962
A soviet offensive missile build-up in Cuba was revealed by President John F. Kennedy who ordered a naval and air quarantine on shipment of offensive military equipment to the island. Kennedy and Soviet Premier Khrushchev reached agreement on 28 Oct, and President Kennedy announced that Soviet missile bases in Cuba were being dismantled.

02 Aug 1964
U.S. destroyers *USS Maddox* and *USS C. Turner Joy* were attacked by North Vietnamese torpedo boats in the Gulf of Tonkin, resulting in Gulf of Tonkin Resolution and a major American commitment.

03 Oct 1964
Operation Sea Orbit, a 64-day-long around the world, unreplenished cruise, involving *USS Bainbridge, USS Long Beach* and *USS Enterprise*, was completed successfully.

08 Jun 1965
U.S. commanders were authorized to commit 23,000 advisors to Vietnam. By year's end, 184,000 servicemen were committed. By 1966, that figure had doubled.

08 Jun 1967
American communication ship *USS Liberty* was attacked by Israeli planes and torpedo boats in international waters off the Sinai Peninsula. 34 crewmen were killed; 75 wounded. Israel apologized for what they termed an accident.

21 Oct 1967
As the fighting and American casualties escalated in Vietnam, large-scale protests against the war erupted in the U.S. Thousands of war protestors marched in Washington, D.C.; hundreds were arrested when they stormed the Pentagon.

23 Jan 1968
USS Pueblo and 83 crew members were seized in the Sea of Japan by North Koreans. All but one were released on 22 DEC.

30 Jan 1968
The "Tet Offensive," when the Vietcong and North Vietnamese attacked 30 provincial capitals in South Vietnam. This led President Johnson to announce a bombing halt over 90 percent of North Vietnam, and he asked Hanoi for a peaceful response.

10 May 1968
Paris Peace Talks begin.

25 Jan 1969
The Navy's first nuclear-powered, deep-submergence research and ocean engineering vehicle, NR-1 was launched. This five-man vessel is capable of operating for weeks at a time at great depths.

15 Apr 1969
American forces in South Vietnam reached a final peak of 543,000. U.S. battle deaths reached 33,641 earlier that month.

08 Jul 1969
U.S. combat troops begin withdrawing from Vietnam.

20 Jul 1969
Former Navy pilot Neil Armstrong became the first man to set foot on the moon.

Alvin, the Navy's first deep-diving vehicle, was successfully tested at 6000-foot depths.

14 Nov 1969
An all-Navy Apollo crew (Commanders Charles Conrad and Richard Gordon and Lieutenant Commander Alan Bean) lifted off from Cape Canaveral on the second lunar expedition.

30 Apr 1970
U.S. and South Vietnam forces invade neutral Cambodia to destroy communist supply bases in border area sanctuaries.

04 May 1970
Four students slain and nine wounded when National Guardsmen open fire at a demonstration against the war at Kent State University.

3-5 May 1970
Massive anti-war demonstrations held in Washington,

D.C. More than 12,000 protestors were arrested—including 7,000 in a single day—a record high for arrests during a civil disturbance in U.S. history.

11 Feb 1971
ADM Elmo Zumwalt, Jr., Chief of Naval Operations, ended the practice of enlisting Filipinos to serve only as stewards in the U.S. Navy. They will now be accepted as seaman recruits and assigned ratings ". . .based on the needs of the service, and the background of the individual."

01 Apr 1971
The Navy announced that the *USS James Madison* (SSBN 627) departed Charleston, South Carolina, for her assigned secret station. She was the first U.S. submarine to go to sea armed with missiles carrying multiple nuclear warheads.

28 Apr 1971
The Navy announced the selection of 49 new rear admirals. Among them were the first black admiral in the Navy, Captain Samuel L. Gravely, Jr., and America's first man in space, Captain Alan B. Shepard, Jr.

14 Jun 1971
The Chief of Naval Operations announced that the enlisted men's uniform would be replaced by an officer-style uniform

08 Aug 1971
The Navy accepted its first rescue submarine—a torpedo-shaped vessel, capable of rescuing crewmen from subs at depths down to 5,000 feet.

08 Oct 1971
The largest U.S. base on the five-and-a-half-million-mile Antarctic continent—McMurdo Station—opened.

07 Nov 1971
Navy Mobile Construction Battalion 5, the last Seabee Unit to serve in Vietnam, arrived at its homeport of Port Hueneme, California, ending the battalion's sixth deployment to the Far East. At the peak of the Vietnam buildup there were 12 Seabee battalions deployed there.

07 Jan 1972
It was announced that the Navy will establish a small communications facility on ten acres of the large British base on the island of Bahrain.

08 Jan 1972
The keel of the *USS Los Angeles* (SSN 688), the first in a new class of attack submarines, was laid at the Newport News Shipbuilding and Drydock Company.

A sentry and his dog on dawn patrol in Da Nang, Vietnam.

08 Aug 1972
Navy announced that it would send women to sea as
regular ship's company officers and crew for the first
time in history. Women would also be allowed to take
almost any job in the Navy. Three days later, Ensign
Rosemary E. Nelson was assigned as the assistant supply
officer, and Lieutenant Junior Grade Ann Kerr was
assigned as personnel officer aboard the hospital ship
USS Sanctuary.

11 Aug 1972
Last U.S. combat troops departed Vietnam.

18 Dec 1972
Peace talks broke down and President Nixon ordered the
heaviest bombing of the war by B-52s. Fifteen were shot
down by Hanoi's surface to air missile batteries.

03 Feb 1973
The Navy, bothered by shipboard personnel disorders,
quietly purged itself of nearly 3,000 trouble-makers —
both black and white — "...whose records reflect
marginal performance or substandard conduct."

12 Feb 1973
The first 116 American prisoners of war released by
North Vietnam received heroes' welcomes when they
arrived at Clark Air Force Base in the Philippines.

29 Mar 1973
Last American troops left Vietnam, officially ending any
direct U.S. involvement. U.S. combat deaths were
counted at 46,079.

22 Jun 1973
Another all Navy crew (Captain Charles Conrad and
Commanders Joseph P. Kerwin and Paul J. Wietz)
splashed down on the first Skylab mission. The team
had set numerous records and accomplished all of its
objectives.

10 Nov 1973
The U.S. Navy's first gas turbine-powered destroyer,
USS Spruance (DD 963) was launched at Ingalls
Shipyard at Pascagoula, Mississippi.

01 Dec 1973
USS Tarawa, the first of five ships in a new class of
amphibious assault ships was launched at Ingalls
Shipyard at Pascagoula, Mississippi.

12 Jul 1974
The President signed legislation making Admiral's
House, the former residence of the Chief of Naval
Operations, the official residence of the Vice President.

16 Sep 1974
The President announced establishment of a clemency
program for draft evaders and deserters who committed
their offenses between 01 Aug 1964 and 28 Mar 1973,
which would provide for issuance of a clemency
discharge following two years of alternate service.

09 Nov 1974
USS Pegasus (PHM 1), the first of a new class of patrol
hydrofoil missile ships, was launched by the Boeing
Company in Seattle, Washington.

10 Apr 1975
In commemoration of the bicentennial of the United
States, the Navy announced plans to name a destroyer in
honor of Admiral Comte Francois de Grasse,
commander of the French fleet which won the decisive
battle of the Chesapeake Capes during the American
Revolution.

29 Apr 1975
Greece and the United States announced they had agreed
to end an agreement providing homeport facilities to
Sixth Fleet ships and to close the U.S. Air Force base near
Athens.

03 May 1975
USS Nimitz (CVN 68) first of a new class of nuclear-
powered aircraft carriers was commissioned at Norfolk,
Virginia.

12 May 1975
The U.S. merchant ship SS Mayaguez, owned by the
Sea-Land Corporation, was fired on and seized by a
Cambodian gunboat in the Gulf of Thailand. Two days
later U.S. Marines carried by the destroyer escort USS
Harold E. Holt boarded and retook the deserted SS
Mayaguez. Other Marines, flown by Air Force
helicopters and supported by naval air and surface
forces, landed at Tang Island in the Gulf of Thailand in
an effort to recover the seized merchant seamen. The
latter, who were not on the island, were returned to their
ship unharmed. Two weeks later, the Defense
Department announced the toll of U.S. servicemen killed
in the recapture of the Mayaguez was 15, of whom 11
were Marines, two were sailors and two were airmen;
three others were listed as missing.

An Air Force HH-43 Huskie rescue helo hovers over a Navy
River Patrol Boat on the Bassac River in Vietnam.

Trident missile launch sequence.

09 SEP 1975
The Navy relieved Commander Connelly D. Stevenson, Commanding Officer of *USS Finback* (SSN 670), because on 10 July he allowed a go-go dancer to perform topless on deck as the submarine sailed out of Port Canaveral, Florida.

15 SEP 1975
The one-year-old clemency program ended after processing about 16,500 applications from an estimated potential 100,000.

18 Nov 1975
The Chief of Naval Operations announced establishment of a Navy Affirmative Action Planning Task Force, "to conduct an in-depth review of the present status of equal opportunity in the Navy and to determine necessary changes to achieve full equal opportunity for all personnel."

22 Nov 1975
USS Belknap (CG 26) collided with *USS John F. Kennedy* (CV 67) while the ships were steaming in the Mediterranean. Six sailors from *Belknap* and one from *Kennedy* were killed in the accident. Repairs to *Belknap* cost $210 million . . . three times the ship's original cost.

10 JAN 1977
Defense Department authorized the Navy to build five 131-foot Fast Patrol Hydrofoil Missile ships (PHMs) as follow-on units to the NATO designed Boeing Company's *USS Pegasus* (PHM 1).

14 JAN 1977
For the first time, an all-nuclear-powered task group operated in both deployed fleets. The Seventh Fleet task group was composed of *USS Enterprise* (CVN 65), *USS Long Beach* (CGN 9) and *USS Truxton* (CGN 35). The Sixth Fleet task group was composed of *USS Nimitz* (CVN 68), *USS California* (CGN 36) and *USS South Carolina* (CGN 39).

18 JAN 1977
The Navy successfully launched the first test flight of the new long range Trident ballistic missile from a test pad at Cape Canaveral.

09 JUL 1977
The missile-armed hydrofoil *USS Pegasus* (PHM1) was commissioned at Seattle, Washington.

04 AUG 1977
Divers, working 220 feet below the surface off Cape Hatteras, completed a 17-day probe of the wreck of *USS Monitor* after recovering artifacts and placing the first men on the Civil War ironclad since she was sunk in a gale 115 years earlier.

27 OCT 1977
The Navy acknowledged the highest enlisted desertion rate in its history during Fiscal Year 1977, with 31.7 desertions per 1,000 enlisted personnel (14,539 desertions out of a total enlisted population of 459,857), or six times the World War II high, and more than double the Vietnam peak.

17 Dec 1977
The first ship of her class of guided missile frigates, *USS Oliver Hazard Perry* was commissioned in Bath, Maine.

26 Jan 1978
The Secretary of the Navy announced the choice of Kings Bay, Georgia, as the site of a new submarine support base for fleet ballistic missile submarines, replacing that of Rota, Spain.

22 Mar 1978
Navy announced plans to homeport four destroyer or frigate type ships at Newport, Rhode Island, beginning in the fall of that year, in order to "improve the strategic dispersal of the Atlantic Fleet." Only reserve force ships had been based in Newport since the regular fleet pullout in 1973.

13 Oct 1978
Captain Joan Bynum, Nurse Corps, became the first black woman to be promoted to the rank of Captain, U.S. Navy, in a ceremony at Yokosuka, Japan.

01 Nov 1978
For the first time in the history of the U.S. Navy, nine women reported for regular sea duty in ships other than hospital or troop transports. The women, all ensigns, reported aboard the Atlantic Fleet ships *USS L.Y. Spear* (AS 36), *USS Vulcan* (AR 5) and *USS Puget Sound* (AD 38); and the Pacific Fleet ships *USS Dixon* (AS 37) and *USS Norton Sound* (AVM 1).

21 Feb 1979
Six U.S. Navy ships were involved in the sea evacuation of 440 people, including 200 U.S. citizens, from the Iranian ports of Bandar Abbas and Char Nahar.

17 Mar 1979
The 14,000-ton American cargo ship *Letitia Lykes* called at Shanghai, People's Republic of China, becoming the first American ship to call at a Red Chinese port since 1949.

07 Apr 1979
The first Trident class nuclear-powered ballistic missile submarine, *USS Ohio*, was launched at Groton, Connecticut, while 3,000 anti-nuclear protestors chanted and sang nearby.

07 Jul 1979
USS Emory S. Land (AS 39), the first submarine tender of her class, was commissioned at Norfolk, Virginia.

28 Jul 1979
USS Arthur W. Radford (DD 968) became the first Sixth Fleet ship to fire a Harpoon missile with an over-the-horizon hit on the exercise target, the former *USS Landsdowne* (DD 486) at a range of 60 miles.

22 Sep 1979
USS Vulcan (AR 5) reported to the Sixth Fleet in the Mediterranean, becoming the first non-hospital ship or transport to deploy with women in the ship's company. *Vulcan's* crew included 55 women.

30 Oct 1979
The first at-sea evaluation of the F-18 Hornet aircraft began aboard *USS America* (CV 66).

10 Jan 1980
Ensign Roberta L. McIntyre, "E" Division Officer and Electrical Officer aboard *USS Dixon* (AS 37), became the Navy's first woman to be designated a Surface Warfare Officer.

01 Mar 1980
The new Rapid Deployment Joint Task Force headquarters was opened at MacDill Air Force Base, Florida.

01 Mar 1980
The Chief of Naval Operations proposed to the Secretary of Defense that the four Iowa-class battleships be modernized and reactivated.

03 Mar 1980
USS Nautilus (SSN 571), the world's first nuclear-powered ship, was decommissioned at Vallejo, California. She later was opened as a museum in New London, Connecticut.

10 May 1980
USS Belknap (CG 26) was recommissioned at the Philadelphia Naval Shipyard. She had been severely damaged by a fire following a collision in the Mediterranean with the *USS John F. Kennedy* on 27 November 1975.

30 Sep 1980
All Naval Districts except Naval District Washington were disestablished. Former naval district functions were transferred to appropriate local or naval base commanders.

01 Oct 1980
USS Saratoga (CV 60) was the first aircraft carrier to undergo the Service Life Extension Program (SLEP) designed to prolong her useful service for up to 16 years. This massive overhaul and upgrade was performed in Philadelphia.

14 Apr 1981
Airman Recruit Paul A. Trerice died of cardiac arrest and heat stroke, while assigned to the correctional custody unit (CCU) on board *USS Ranger* (CV 61) moored at Subic Bay in the Philippines. His death touched off an investigation into allegations by a former *Ranger* crewmate of maltreatment and physical abuse in *Ranger's* brig and CCU.

Open House aboard *USS Intrepid.*

27 Apr 1981
The Navy officially transferred the aircraft carrier *USS Intrepid* (ex-CVS 11) to the Intrepid Museum Foundation for conversion to a Sea-Air-Space Museum at New York City.

03 Jun 1981
Navy Secretary John Lehman announced the establishment of a Council on Review and Oversight for top management attention to reduce fraud, waste and abuse.

02 Apr 1982
The Argentine governing junta announced that army, navy and air force units had captured British-held Falkland Islands. After more than two months of intense fighting, Great Britain's victory was complete on 20 JUN, following capture of the South Sandwich Islands.

01 Jan 1983
A new unified command for Southwest Asia, known as the U.S. Central Command, was activated. The new command, made up of units of all services, is responsible for protecting U.S. security interests in the Middle East, Persian Gulf and Indian Ocean areas. The command took the place of the Rapid Deployment Joint Task Force and is empowered to draw from a pool of 230,000 troops in the United States.

22 Jan 1983
The first of a class of AEGIS guided missile cruisers, *USS Ticonderoga* was commissioned at Pascagoula, Mississippi.

29 Jul 1983
The Secretary of the Navy announced that the Navy had selected Stapleton, Staten Island, New York, as the "preferred alternative" homeport for a surface action group including the battleship *USS Iowa*, four other combatants, plus two reserve frigates.

01 Sep 1983
The Soviet Air Force shot down a Korean Air Lines Boeing 747 airliner off the Kamchatka Peninsula. All 269 persons on board the plane died, including 61 Americans. Navy ships and aircraft became heavily involved in the search and rescue operations which continued through heavy seas and harsh weather until 05 November.

21 Oct 1983
Tragedy struck the Marine Barracks at Beirut International Airport. A terrorist drove an explosives-laden truck into a building where Marines and other servicemen were sleeping and blew it up. The final toll of dead: 220 Marines, 18 sailors and three soldiers.

Left, the battleship *USS New Jersey* rests in drydock at the Philadelphia Naval Shipyard; above, the AEGIS cruiser *USS Vincennes* is towed into drydock.

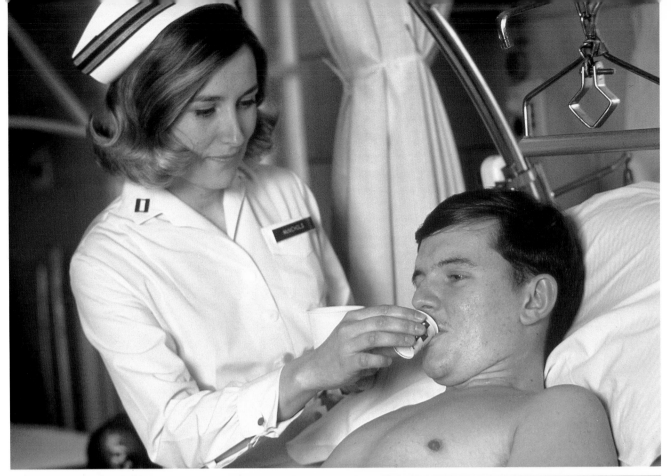

Top left, a Navy nurse provides medication to a patient in the neuro-surgery ward at the National Naval Medical Center; bottom left, "Med lights" brighten an aircraft carrier at rest; right, Bob Hope is a best friend and supporter to sailors deployed to the Seven Seas; below, the Vietnam Memorial and the Washington Monument are joined by a new, important landmark in the United States Navy Memorial on Pennsylvania Avenue.

23 Oct 1983
The governments of the Association of East Caribbean Nations requested U.S. assistance in ensuring the safety of foreigners living in Grenada and in restoring order there. The quick and complete success achieved in securing the island and helping to provide a basis for restoral of a popularly chosen government reflect well on the Navy's flexibility and responsiveness. The final casualty list totaled 18 U.S. servicemen killed and 116 wounded.

25 Oct 1983
A Navy and Marine amphibious force and Army airborne units, backed by a carrier battle group, invaded Marxist Grenada to rescue a thousand American medical students and halt the drift of that tiny Caribbean island into the Soviet-Cuban orbit. The main opposition ashore came from Cuban "construction workers" and military reservists.

02 Nov 1983
The United States declared hostilities in Grenada ended and began withdrawing troops. The battle group with *USS Independence* and a five-ship amphibious group departed the area.

28 Dec 1983
Carrier-based aircraft attacked Syrian anti-aircraft missile sites. Two aircraft, an A-6 and an A-7, were lost. The A-6 pilot was killed and his navigator captured and later released unharmed.

08 Feb 1984
USS New Jersey (BB 62) is credited with silencing the hills of Beirut, Lebanon, after her incessant, effective shore bombardment using 16-inch guns.

28 Apr 1984
USS Iowa (BB 61) is recommissioned in Pascagoula, Mississippi.

24 Jan 1985
The Space shuttle Discovery was launched from Cape Canaveral on the first secret all-military space mission reported to be for the positioning of a 5,000 pound electronic reconnaissance satellite. The mission was commanded by Captain Thomas K. Mattingly, USN.

20 May 1985
Retired Navy Chief John A. Walker, Jr. was arrested for attempting to pass classified documents to Russian agents. Two days later, his son, Michael L. Walker, was seized aboard the aircraft carrier *USS Nimitz* and charged with espionage. A week later, a third Walker family member, retired LCDR Arthur J. Walker was arrested in Virginia Beach and charged with espionage.

28 May 1985
Ex-*USS Nautilus* went to sea for the last time. The 30-year-old nuclear submarine began a voyage from Mare Island, California, to New London, Connecticut, where she was placed on permanent display.

14 Jun 1985
TransWorld Airlines flight 847 was seized by terrorists just after takeoff from Athens airport. Steelworker Second Class (Diver) Robert D. Stethem, a member of Norfolk-based Underwater Construction Team One, was killed in the hijacking.

16 Jun 1985
USS Avenger, the first of a new class of mine countermeasure ships, was launched by Peterson Builders, in Sturgeon Bay, Wisconsin.

17 Jun 1985
A task force of seven Navy ships carrying 100 aircraft and 1,800 Marines sailed toward the Eastern Mediterranean and Lebanon as a show of force.

07 Oct 1985
Four Palestinian terrorists seized the Italian-flag cruise ship *Achille Lauro* in the Mediterranean. Navy F-14 fighters flying from *USS Saratoga* (CV 60) forced down the aircraft carrying the hijackers to Tunisia, permitting Italian authorities to board the aircraft on its arrival at Sigonella Naval Air Station, Sicily.

06 May 1986
Nuclear attack submarines *USS Ray* (SSN 653), *USS Hawkbill* (SSN 666) and *USS Archerfish* (SSN 678) became the first three submarines ever to surface simultaneously at the North Pole.

13 May 1986
The first overseas deployment of a battleship battle group.

04 Jul 1986
USS Iowa (BB 61) was the official reviewing ship for the Fifth International Naval Review in New York Harbor. The President and First Lady were embarked for the ceremony conducted in commemoration of the Statue of Liberty Centennial. In all, 35 Navy ships representing 18 nations participated in the four-day event.

25 Oct 1986
USS Theodore Roosevelt (CVN 71), the Navy's newest aircraft carrier, was commissioned at Newport News Shipbuilding, coincident to the shipyard's 100th anniversary.

5-11 Nov 1986
USS Reeves (CG 24), *USS Oldendorf* (DD 972) and *USS Rentz* (FFG 46) made an historic port visit to Qingdao, People's Republic of China; the first naval ship visit to PRC since WW II.

17 May 1987
The guided missile frigate *USS Stark* was struck by two Iraqi sea-skimming Exocet missiles while operating in the Persian Gulf. Thirty-seven sailors were killed in the attack. This incident raised questions regarding deficiencies in Navy's fire fighting and damage control capabilities.

12 Sep 1987
USS Avenger (MCM 1) first of a new class of mine countermeasure ships, and the first new ship with minesweeping capabilities in the Navy's inventory in more than three decades, was commissioned at Sturgeon Bay, Wisconsin.

13 Oct 1987
On our Navy's 212th Birthday, the United States Navy Memorial was dedicated in Washington, D.C. Its central, prestigious location on Pennsylvania Avenue made the Memorial a new landmark overnight.

—JWA

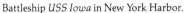

Battleship *USS Iowa* in New York Harbor.

Know the Ropes

*Scuttlebutt has it that if you gundeck your work and spend all
of your time skylarking, instead of minding your Ps and Qs,
then you'll end up in the horse latitudes and will never know the ropes.
Get some geedunk and enjoy reading about the origin of these
and some other famous Navy expressions.*

WHEN WE SAY someone knows the ropes, we infer that he knows his way around at sea, and is quite capable of handling most nautical problems. Through the years, the meaning of the phrase has changed somewhat. Originally, the statement was printed on a seaman's discharge to indicate that he knew the names and primary uses of the main ropes on board ship. In other words, "This man is a novice seaman and knows only the basics of seamanship." Learning these basics kept many a young sailor's stomach in knots.

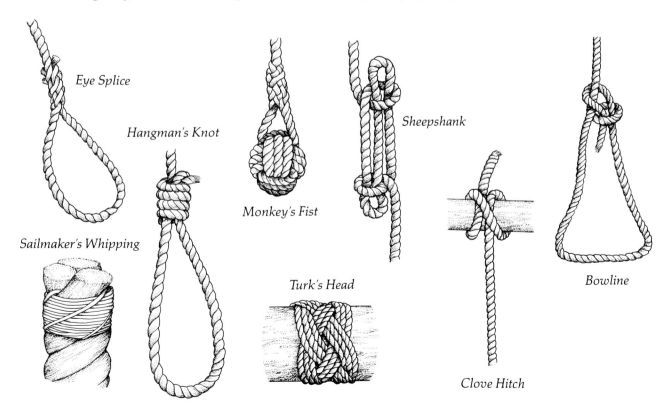

Eye Splice

Hangman's Knot

Sailmaker's Whipping

Monkey's Fist

Turk's Head

Sheepshank

Clove Hitch

Bowline

Gundecking

IN THE MODERN NAVY, falsifying reports, records, and the like is often referred to as "gundecking." The origin of the term is somewhat obscure, but at the risk of gundecking, here are two plausible explanations for its modern usage.

The deck below the upper deck on British sailing ships-of-war was called the gundeck although it carried no guns. This false deck may have been constructed to deceive enemies as to the amount of armament carried, thus the gundeck was a falsification.

A more plausible explanation may stem from shortcuts taken by early midshipmen when doing their navigation lessons. Each mid was supposed to take sun lines at noon and star sights at night and then go below to the gundeck, work out their calculations and show them to the navigator.

Certain of these young men, however, had a special formula for getting the correct answers. They would note the noon, or last position, on the quarterdeck traverse board and determine the approximate current position by dead reconing plotting. Armed with this information, they proceeded to the gundeck to "gundeck" their navigation homework by simply working backwards from the dead reconing position.

Scuttlebutt

THE ORIGIN OF THE WORD "scuttlebutt," which is nautical parlance for a rumor, comes from a combination of "scuttle," to make a hole in the ship's side causing her to sink, and "butt," a cask or hogshead used in the days of wooden ships to hold drinking water. Thus, the term scuttlebutt means a cask with a hole in it. "Scuttle" describes what most rumors accomplish if not to the ship, at least to morale. "Butt' describes the water cask where men naturally congregated, and that's where most rumors get started. The terms "galley yarn" and "messdeck intelligence" also mean the spreading of rumors and many, of course, start on the messdeck.

Log Book

TODAY, ANY BOUND RECORD kept on a daily basis aboard ship is called a "log." Originally, records were kept on the sailing ships by inscribing information onto shingles cut from logs and hinged so they opened like books. When paper became more readily available, "log books" were manufactured from paper and bound. Shingles were relegated to naval museums—but the slang term stuck.

Ship's Husband

SOMETIMES WHEN A SHIP is heading for the yards, an old salt says that she is going to her husband. Used now, it causes novices to wonder what he's talking about. A ship's husband was once a widely used term which described the man in charge of the shipyard responsible for the repair of a particular ship. It was not uncommon to hear the sailors of creaky ships lament, "Ah, she's been a good ship, lads, but she's needing her husband now."

In the course of a ship's life, she may have had more than one husband but this had little bearing upon her true affections. Traditions has it, her love was saved solely for her sailors.

Carry On

IN THE DAYS OF SAIL, the officer of the deck kept a weather eye constantly on the slightest change in wind so sail could be reefed or added as necessary to ensure the fastest headway. Whenever a good breeze came along, the order to "carry on" would be given. It meant to hoist every bit of canvas the yards could carry. Pity the poor sailor whose weather eye failed him and the ship was caught partially reefed when a good breeze arrived.

Through the centuries the term's connotation has changed somewhat. Today, the Bluejackets Manual defines "carry on" as an order to resume work; work not so grueling as two centuries ago.

Boatswain, Cockswain, Skiffswain

As REQUIRED by 17th century law, British ships-of-war carried three smaller boats—the boat, the cock boat, and the skiff. The boat, or gig, was usually used by the captain to go ashore and was the larger of the three. The cock boat was a very small rowboat used as a ship's tender. The skiff was a lightweight all-purpose vessel. The suffix "swain" means keeper, thus the keepers of the boat, cock and skiff were called boatswain, cockswain and skiffswain respectively. Until 1949, a boatswain's mate 3rd class in the Navy was called a cockswain.

Navy Blue

BLUE HAS NOT ALWAYS BEEN "navy blue." In fact, it wasn't until 1745 that the expression navy blue meant anything at all.

In that year, several British officers petitioned the Admiralty for adaption of new uniforms for its officers. The first lord requested several officers to model various uniforms under consideration so he could select the best. He then selected several uniforms of various styles and colors to present to George II for the final decision.

King George, unable to decide on either style or color, finally chose a blue and white uniform because they were the favorite color combinations of the first lord's wife, Duchess of Bedford.

Mind Your Ps and Qs

THERE ARE FEW OF US have not at one time or another been admonished to "mind our Ps and Qs," or in other words, to behave our best. Oddly enough, "mind your Ps and Qs" had nautical beginnings as a method of keeping books on the waterfront.

In the days of sail, when sailors were paid a pittance, seamen drank their ale in taverns whose keepers were willing to extend credit until payday. Since many salts were illiterate, keepers kept a talley of pints and quarts consumed by each sailor on a chalkboard behind the bar. Next to each person's name, a mark was made under "P" for pint, or "Q" for quart, whenever a seaman ordered another draught.

On payday, each seaman was liable for each mark next to his name, so he was forced to "mind his Ps and Qs" or get into financial trouble. To ensure an accurate count by unscrupulous keepers, sailors had to keep their wits and remain somewhat sober. Sobriety usually ensured good behavior, hence the meaning of "mind your Ps and Qs."

Bokoo

OFTEN AN OLD SALT will boast that he has had bokoo this or has done something bokoo times during his seafaring years. The picturesque sound of the word "bokoo" may cause one to wonder how it came to mean "many" or "alot."

Actually, bokoo is a legitimate French word, "beaucoup," meaning "very many." Americanization changed the spelling and pronunciation but the meaning remains unchanged. Like many foreign terms that have crept into our nautical lingo, "bokoo" is the inevitable product of generations of American seamen meeting peoples of other nations and adopting bokoo phrases from their languages for everyday shipboard use.

Yankee

AMERICANS ARE KNOWN by their nicknames from Hong Kong to Timbukto; one of the most widely used is "Yankee." Its origin is uncertain, but its is believed to have been given us by the early Dutch.

Early American sea captains were known, but not revered, for their ability to drive a hard bargain. Dutchmen, also regarded as extremely frugal, jokingly referred to the hard-to-please Americans as "Yankers," or wranglers, and the nom de plume persists to this day.

Midshipmen

"MIDSHIPMEN" originally referred to the youngsters aboard British Navy vessels who were in training to become naval officers. Their primary duties included carrying orders from the officers, quartered in the stern, to the crew, quartered in the fo'c'sle. The repeated scampering through the middle part of the ship earned them the name "midshipmen" and the nickname "middle."

Naval Academy students and Navy Reserve Officer Training Candidates are still called midshipmen because, just like their counterparts of old, they are in training to become officers in the sea service. It is interesting to note that mids (the term middie went out of use only recently) back in the days of sail could begin their naval careers at the ripe old age of eight.

Show a Leg

MANY OF OUR NAVY'S colorful expressions originated as practical means of communicating vital information. One such expression is "show a leg."

In the British Navy of King George III and earlier, many sailors' wives accompanied them on long voyages. This practice caused a multitude of problems, but some ingenious bosun solved one that tended to make reveille a hazardous event: that of distinguishing which bunks held males and which held females.

To avoid dragging the wrong "mates" out of the rack, the bosun asked all to "show a leg." If the leg shown was adorned with silk, the owner was allowed to continue sleeping. if the leg was hairy and tattooed, the owner was forced to "turn-to."

In today's Navy, showing a leg is a signal to the reveille petty officer that you have heard his call and are awake.

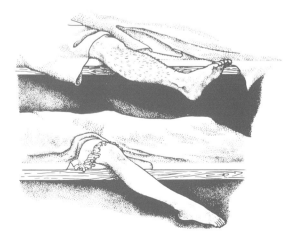

Boatswain's Pipe

No self-respecting boatswain's mate would dare admit he couldn't blow his pipe in a manner above reproach. This pipe, which is the emblem of the boatswain and his mates, has an ancient and interesting history.

On the ancient row-galleys, the boatswain used his pipe to "call the stroke." Later because its shrill tune could be heard above most of the activity on board, it was used to signal various happenings such as knock-off and the boarding of officials. So essential was this signaling device to the well-being of the ship, that it became a badge of office and honor in the British and American Navy of the sailing ships.

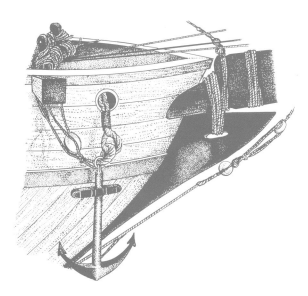

Horse Latitudes

The words of Samuel Taylor Coleridge, "Idle as a painted ship upon a painted ocean" well describe a sailing ship's situation when it entered the horse latitudes. Located near the West Indies between 30 and 40 degrees north latitude, these waters were noted for unfavorable winds that becalmed cattle ships heading from Europe to America.

Often ships carrying horses would have to cast several overboard to conserve drinking water for the rest as the ship rode out the unfavorable winds. Because so many horses and other cattle were tossed to the sea, the area came to be known as the "horse latitudes."

In Through the Hawsepipe

Sometimes we hear an old chief petty officer claim he came into the Navy through the hawsepipe and it makes one wonder if he is referring to some early enlistment program. Actually, it was an enlistment program of sorts; it means a person is salty and savvies the ways of the sea because he began his nautical career on the lowest ladder of the deck force. A hawsepipe or hawsehole, incidentally, is a hole in the bow of the ship through which the anchor chain runs.

Bitter End

As any able-bodied seaman can tell you, a turn of a line around a bitt, those wooden or iron posts sticking through a ship's deck, is called a bitter. Thus, the last of the line secured to the bitts is known as the bitter end. Nautical usage has somewhat expanded the original definition in that today the end of any line, secured to bitts or not, is called a bitter end.

The landlubbing phrases "stick to the bitter end" and "faithful to the bitter end" are derivations of the nautical term and refer to anyone who insists on adhering to a course of action without regard to consequences.

Chit

One tradition carried on in the Navy is the use of the "chit." It is a carry over from the days when Hindu traders used slips of paper called "citthi" for money, so they wouldn't have to carry heavy bags of gold and silver.

British sailors shortened the word to chit and applied it to their mess vouchers. Its most outstanding use in the Navy today is for drawing pay, and a form used for requesting leave and liberty. But the term is currently applied to almost any piece of paper from a pass to an official letter requesting some privilege.

Ditty Bags

DITTY BAG (or box) was originally called "ditto bag" because it contained at least two of everything: two needles, two spools of thread, two buttons, etc. With the passing of years, the "ditto" was dropped in favor of "ditty" and remains so today.

Before World War I, the Navy issued ditty boxes made of wood and styled after foot lockers. These carried the personal gear and some clothes of the sailor.

Today, the ditty bag is still issued to recruits and contains a sewing kit, toiletry articles, and personal items such as writing paper and pens.

Smoking Lamp

SEA DOGS WHO SAILED the wooden ships endured hardships that sailors today never suffer. Cramped quarters, poor, unpalatable food, bad lighting, and boredom were hard facts of sea life. But perhaps a more frustrating problem was getting fire to kindle a cigar or pipe tobacco after a hard day's work.

Matches were scarce and unreliable, yet smoking contributed positively to the morale of the crew so oil lamps were hung in the fo'c'sle and used as matches. Smoking was restricted to certain times of the day by the bos'un's. When it was allowed, the "smoking lamps" were "lighted" and the men relaxed with their tobacco.

Fire was, and still is, the great enemy of ships at sea. The smoking lamp was centrally located for the convenience of all and was the only authorized light aboard. It was a practical way of keeping open flames away from the magazines and other storage areas.

In the Navy today, the smoking lamps have disappeared, but the words "smoking lamp is lighted in all authorized spaces" remains, a carryover from our past.

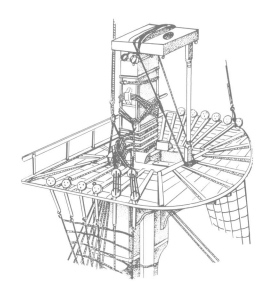

Crow's Nest

THE CROW (the bird, not the rating badge) was an essential part of the early sailors' navigation equipment. These land-lubbing fowl were carried on board to help the navigator determine where the closest land lay when the weather prevented sighting the shore visually. In cases of poor visibility, a crow was released and the navigator plotted a course that corresponded with the bird's because it invariably headed toward land.

The crow's nest was situated high in the main mast where the look-out stood his watch. Often, he shared this lofty perch with a crow or two since the crows' cages were kept there: hence the "crow's nest."

Master-at-Arms

THE MASTER-AT-ARMS rating is by no means a modern innovation. Naval records show that these "sheriffs of the sea" were keeping order as early as the reign of Charles I of England. At that time, they were charged with keeping the swords, pistols, carbines, and muskets in good working order as well as ensuring that the bandoliers were filled with fresh powder before combat.

Besides being chiefs of police at sea, the sea corporals, as they were called in the British Navy, had to be qualified in close order fighting under arms and able to train seamen in hand-to-hand combat. In the days of sail, the MAAs were truly "masters at arms." The master-at-arms in the U.S. Navy can trace the beginning of his rate to the Union Navy of the Civil War.

Sally Ship

"SALLY SHIP" WAS NOT A SHIP but a method of lossing a vessel run aground from the mud holding her fast. In the days before sophisticated navigation equipment, ships ran aground much more often than today. A grounded ship could be freed with little or no hull damage if she could be rocked out of her muddy predicament.

To free her, the order was given to "sally ship." The crew gathered in a line along one side and then ran athwartships from port to starboard and back and forth until the vessel began to roll. Often the rolling broke the mud's suction and she could be pulled free and gotten underway.

Bell Bottom Trousers

THESE WIDE-LEGGED PANTS went out with the jaunty white hats worn by sailors in the U.S. Navy until 1975. They were cut with a flare in the legs for several reasons: They were easier to roll up, as when a man was swabbing decks; but primarily the flare permitted sailors to remove the trousers quickly without removing their shoes first. This was a safety feature in case their ship sank or they were knocked overboard. In such instances, sailors were taught to tie a knot in each pant leg, force air into the trousers through the top, thus making a natural air pocket . . . life preserver.

Dungarees

WEBSTER DEFINES dungaree as "a coarse kind of fabric worn by the poorer class of people and also used for *tents and sail.*" We find it hard to picture our favorite pair of dungarees flying from the mast of a sailing ship, but in those days sailors often made both their working clothes and hammocks out of discarded sail cloth.

The cloth used then wasn't as well woven nor was it dyed blue, but it served the purpose. Dungarees worn by sailors of the Continental Navy were cut directly from old sails and remained tan in color just as they had been when filled with wind.

After battles, it was the practice in both the American and British navies for captains to report more sail lost in battle than actually was the case so the crew would have cloth to mend their hammocks and make new clothes. Since the cloth was called dungaree, clothes made from the fabric borrowed the name.

Charley Noble

THE ENLISTED MAN'S NAME for the galley smoke stack or funnel is Charley Noble. The funnel is said to have been named after a stern old merchant captain who discovered that the galley's smokestack was made of copper and therefore should receive a daily polishing. In today's Navy, it is the custom to send green recruits to find Charley Noble, a hunt which causes endless amusement for the ship's veterans.

Chaplains

CHAPLAINS, the military men of the cloth, are rightly named according to French legend.

It seems that Saint Martin of Tours shared his cloak—by splitting it in half—with a beggar on a wintry day at the gates of Amiens, France. The cloak was preserved since it was believed to have been shared with Christ, and became the sacred banner of French kings. The officer tasked with the care of the cloak and carrying into battle was called the chaplain or cloak bearer. Chaplain comes from the French word "chapele," meaning a short cloak. Later, priests or chaplains, rather than field officers, were charged with the care of the sacred cloak.

Chaplains served aboard warships of many nations and in the British and American navies they collected four pence per month from each member of the crew. In return, they rewarded every seaman who learned a psalm by giving him six pence.

Besides holding divine services, chaplains were charged with the instruction of midshipmen and the moral guidance of officers and men alike.

It wasn't until the 18th century that chaplains were permitted to dine in the wardroom. Previously, they messed in their own cabins, although they were frequently invited to dine with the captain.

Sickbay

IN THE MODERN NAVY, sickbay is the place a sailor can receive medical attention. In the days of sail, there were few such places on shore designated specifically for ill seamen, but onboard most ships there were sick berths located in the rounded stern. The contour of the stern suggested the shape of a bay and consequently the sailors began calling the ancient dispensaries sickbays.

Spinning a Yarn

SALTS AND LANDLUBBERS alike delight in hearing a tall tale told with all the trimmings by someone with a talent for "spinning a yarn." While today "spinning a yarn" refers to any exaggerated story, originally it was exclusively a nautical term understood by sailors only.

Officers and mates in the old Navy were stern disciplinarians who believed if sailors were allowed to congregate and tell sea stories, no work would be done. However, there was one job that required congregating on a weekly basis—unraveling the strands of old line.

On this day, the salts could talk to their heart's content and the period came to be known as the time for "spinning yarns." Later anyone telling a tale was said to be "spinning a yarn," a cherished naval tradition.

Jacob's Ladder

A JACOB'S LADDER is a portable ladder made of rope or metal and used primarily as an aid in boarding ship. Originally, the jacob's ladder was a network of line leading to the skysail on wooden ships. The name alludes to the biblical Jacob reputed to have dreamed that he climbed a ladder to the sky.

Anyone who has ever tried climbing a jacob's ladder while carrying a seabag can appreciate the allusion. It does seem that the climb is long enough to take one into the next world.

Pea Coat

SAILORS WHO HAVE TO ENDURE pea-soup weather often don their pea coats but the coat's name isn't derived from the weather.

The heavy topcoat worn in cold, miserable weather by seafaring men was once tailored from pilot cloth—a heavy, coarse, stout kind of twilled blue cloth with the nap on one side. The cloth was sometimes called P-cloth for the initial letter of the word and the garment made from it was called a p-jacket—later a pea coat. The term has been used since 1723 to denote coats made from that cloth.

Skylarking

ORIGINALLY, skylarking described the antics of young Navymen who climbed and slid down the backstays for fun. Since the ancient word "lac" means "to play" and the games started high in the masts, the term was "skylacing." Later, corruption of the word changed it to "skylarking."

Skylarking is a familiar term to most sailors and a popular pastime for others. Today, it is generally looked upon with disfavor while on board ship because "goofing off" can cause accidents and wastes time. However, skylarking wasn't always viewed unfavorably. Back in the days of wooden ships, it was thought to be the better "occupation" of sailors with free time on their hands—skylarking on the weatherdeck—rather than engaging in mutinous talk in a ship's dark corners.

Captain's Mast

THE TERM "MAST" refers to the ceremony that takes place when the captain awards non-judicial punishment for regulation infractions or official recognition for "jobs well done." In the days of sail, ceremonies were held under the mainmast on a regular basis and usually on a Sunday morning just before divine services. Consequently, the ceremony came to be known as "mast" in recognition of the locality of the presentation.

Sideboys

The use of sideboys is a custom inherited from the British Navy. In the days of sail, gangways weren't frequently used so sailors boarded ship by climbing the rope ladders. Important persons were granted the privilege of wrestling with the jacob's ladder. Very important persons, many of whom were rather hefty or aged, were hoisted aboard in a bos'un's chair.

The officer of the deck instructed the bosuns to rig a chair hoist from a yardarm and, with much heaving and hoeing, the VIPs were hoisted aboard much like casks of salt horse. The men who did the hoisting were called sideboys.

Today, sailors lined up in clean uniforms on the quarterdeck when visiting dignitaries embark, are still called sideboys, preserving another naval tradition.

Sea Chanties

Sea chanties were songs sung in the days of sail by crews as they worked at heaving the lines or turning the capstan. The songs' rhythms caused everyone to push or pull simultaneously, hence causing a concerted effort and better results.

Some believe the term is a derivation of the French word "chanter" which means "to sing." Others maintain the spelling should be "shanties," claiming the name refers to the shanties along the Mobile, Alabama, waterfront where many of the tunes were learned by sailors.

Whatever the origin, chanties were divided into three distinct classes. Short-drag chanties, used when a few strong pulls were needed; long-drag chanties, longer songs to speed the work of long-haul jobs; and heaving chanties, used for jobs requiring continuous action such as turning the capstan.

One man, the chanty-man, stood high above the working crew and sang the main lines while the rest of the crew added their voices strongly on the second line. On the last word, a combined pull made the ropes "come home."

A good chanty-man was highly prized by officers and crew alike. Although he had no official title or rate, he was usually relieved of all duties to compose new verses for sea chanties.

Geedunk

To most sailors, the word geedunk means ice cream, candy, potato chips and other assorted snacks—or even the place where they can be purchased. No one, however, knows for certain where the term originated. There are several plausible theories:

In the 1920s, a comic strip character named Harold Teen and his friends spent a great amount of time at Pop's candy store. The store's name was the Sugar Bowl, but Harold and company always called it the geedunk for reasons never explained.

The Chinese word meaning a place of idleness sounds something like "gee dung."

"Geedunk" is the sound made by a vending machine when it dispenses a soft drink in a cup.

It may be derived from the German word "tunk" meaning to dip or sop either in gravy or coffee. Dunking was a common practice in days when bread, not always obtained fresh, needed a bit of "tunking" to soften it. The "ge" is a German unaccented prefix denoting repetition. In time it may have changed from getunk to geedunk.

Whatever theory we use to explain geedunk's origin, it doesn't alter the fact that Navy people are glad it all got started!

Bully Boys

Bully boys, a term prominent in Navy chanties and poems, means in its strictest sense, "beef eating sailors." Sailors of the Colonial Navy had a daily menu of an amazingly elastic substance called bully beef, actually beef jerky. The item appeared so frequently on the messdeck that it naturally lent its name to the sailors who had to eat it.

As an indication of the beef's texture and chewability, it was also called "salt junk," alluding to the rope yarn used for caulking the ship's seams.

Wardroom

Aboard 18th century British ships there was a compartment called the wardrobe and used for storing booty taken at sea. The officers' mess and staterooms were situated nearby, so when the wardrobe was empty they congregated there to take their meals and pass the time.

When the days of swashbuckling and pirating had ended, the wardrobe was used exclusively as an officers' mess and lounge. Having been elevated from a closet to a room, it was called the wardroom.

Dead Horse

BRITISH SEAMAN, apt to be ashore and unemployed for considerable periods between voyages, generally preferred to live in boarding houses near the piers while waiting for sailing ships to take on crews. During these periods of unrestricted liberty, many ran out of money so the innkeepers carried them on credit until hired for another voyage.

When a seaman was booked on a ship, he was customarily advanced a month's wages, if needed, to pay off his boarding house debt. Then, while paying back the ship's master, he worked for nothing but "salt horse" the first several weeks aboard.

Salt horse was the staple diet of early sailors and it wasn't exactly tasty cuisine. Consisting of a low quality beef that had been heavily salted, the salt horse was tough to chew and even harder to digest.

When the debt had been repaid, the salt horse was said to be dead and it was a time for great celebration among the crew. Usually, an effigy of a horse was constructed from odds and ends, set afire and then cast afloat to the cheers and hilarity of the ex-debters.

Today, just as in the days of sail, "dead horse" refers to a debt to the government for advance pay. Sailors today don't burn effigies when the debt is paid but they are no less jubilant than their counterparts of old.

Bamboozle

IN TODAY'S NAVY, when you intentionally deceive someone, usually as a joke, you are said to have bamboozled them. The word was used in the days of sail, also, but the intent was not hilarity. Bamboozle meant to deceive a passing vessel as to your ship's origin or nationality by flying an ensign other than your own—a common practice of pirates.

Tonnage

TODAY, tonnage refers to a ship's displacement in the water or the gross pounds of cargo it is capable of carrying. In the days of sail, this was not so. Tonnage was spelled "tunnage" and referred to the number of "tuns" a ship could carry. A "tun" was a barrel normally used for transporting wine, and tunnage specified the number of barrels that would fit into the ship's hold.

Took the Wind Out of His Sails

OFTEN WE USE "took the wind out of his sails" to describe besting an opponent in an argument. It simply means that one noble adversary presented such a sound argument that his worthy opponent was unable to continue the verbal pugilistics.

Originally, the term described a battle maneuver of sailing vessels. One ship would pass close to windward usually ahead of another, and thereby blanket or rob the breeze from the enemy's canvas, causing him to lose headway.

Fathom

FATHOM WAS ORIGINALLY a land measuring term derived from the Anglo Saxon word "faetm," meaning literally the embracing arms or to embrace. In those days, most measurements were based on average sizes of parts of the body such as the hand or foot, or were derived from average lengths between two points on the body. A fathom is the average distance from fingertip to fingertip of the outstretched arms of a man, about six feet.

Even today in our nuclear Navy, sailors can be seen guesstimating" the length of the line by using the Anglo Saxon fingertip methods; crude but still reliable. And every housewife measuring cloth today knows that from the tip of her nose to the tips of her fingers of one outstretched arm equals one yard.

Rope Yarn Sunday

ON THE DAY the tailor boarded a sailing ship in port, the crew knocked off early, broke out rope yarn and mended clothes and hammocks. One afternoon per week at sea, usually a Wednesday, was reserved for mending. Since it was an afternoon for rest from the usual chores, much like Sunday, it was dubbed "rope yarn Sunday."

The Navy adhered to the custom up to the years immediately after World War II. Men used Wednesday afternoon for personal errands like picking up their laundry and getting haircuts. Of course, they paid back the time by working a half-day on Saturdays.

Today, uniforms require less attention, so rope yarn Sunday has been turned to other purposes; mainly early liberty or a time for catching up on sleep. Some, however, still adhere to tradition and break out the ditty bag for an afternoon of uniform PMS.

Dog Watch

DOG WATCH IS THE NAME given to the 1600-1800 and the 1800-2000 watches aboard ship. The 1600-2000 four-hour watch was originally split to prevent men from always having to stand the same watches daily. As a result, sailors dodge the same daily routine, hence they are dodging the watch or standing the dodge watch.

In its corrupted form, dodge became dog and the procedure is referred to as "dogging the watch" or standing the "dog watch."

Bumboats

IN SPITE OF THEIR NAME, bumboats are not waterborne geedunks piloted by bums or hobos. They are small boats used by native hucksters and gizmo salesmen to transport their wares to ships anchored in the storm. The name is a hand-me-down from "boomboats," as the craft were once permitted to tie up to the boat boom of a ship. An early Low German spelling was "bumboat" and in that form it was taken up by American sailors.

Ensign

THE NAME GIVEN the Navy's junior most officer dates to medieval times. Lords honored their squires by allowing them to carry the ensign (banner) into battle. Later these squires became known by the name of the banner itself.

In the U.S. Army, the lowest ranking officer was originally called "ensign" because he, like the squire of old, would one day lead troops into battle and was training to that end. It is still the lowest commissioned rank in the British army today.

When the U.S. Navy was established, the Americans carried on the tradition and adapted the rank of ensign as the title for its junior commissioned officers.

Keelhaul

TO BE KEELHAULED today is merely to be given a severe reprimand for some infraction of the rules. As late as the 19th century, however, it meant the extreme. It was a dire and often fatal torture employed to punish offenders of certain naval laws.

An offender was securely bound both hand and foot and heavy weights attached to his body. He was then lowered over the ship's side and slowly dragged along under the ship's hull. If he didn't drown—which was rare—barnacles usually ripped him, causing him to bleed to death.

All navies stopped this cruel and unusual punishment many years ago, and today any such punishment is forbidden.

Knot

THE TERM KNOT, or nautical mile, is used world-wide to denote one's speed through water. Today, we measure knots with electronic devices, but 200 years ago such devices were unknown. Ingenious mariners devised a speed measuring device both easy to use and reliable: the "log line." From this method we get the term "knot."

The log line was a length of twine marked at 47.33-foot intervals by colored knots. At one end was fastened a log chip; it was shaped like the sector of a circle and weighted at the rounded end with lead.

When thrown over the stern, it would float pointing upward and would remain relatively stationary. The log line was allowed to run free over the side for 28 seconds and then hauled on board. Knots which had passed over the side were counted. In this way the ship's speed was measured.

Devil to Pay

TODAY THE EXPRESSION "devil to pay" is used primarily as a means of conveying an unpleasant and impending happening. Originally, this expression denoted a specific task aboard ship such as caulking the ship's longest seam.

The "devil" was the longest seam on the wooden ship, and caulking was done with "pay" or pitch. This grueling task of paying the devil was despised by every seaman and the expression came to denote any unpleasant task.

Admiral

AN ADMIRAL is the senior ranking flag officer in the U.S. Navy, but his title comes from the name given the senior ranking officer in the Moorish army of many years ago. A Moorish chief was an "emir," and the chief of all chiefs was an "emir-al." Our English word is derived directly from the Moorish.

Portholes

SOMETIMES, novice seamen will ask "how come holes on the starboard side are called portholes instead of starboardholes?" Many old salts are ready with explanations, but actually the name "porthole" has nothing to do with its location. The word originated during the reign of Henry VI of England (1485). It seems the good king insisted on mounting guns too large for his ships and therefore the conventional methods of securing the weapons on the forecastle and aftcastle could not be used.

A French shipbuilder named James Baker was commissioned to solve the problem. And solve it he did by piercing the ship's sides so the cannon could be mounted inside the fore and after castles. Covers—gun ports—were fitted for heavy weather and when the cannon were not in use.

The French word "porte," meaning door, was used to designate the revolutionary invention. "Porte" was Anglicized to "port" and later corrupted to porthole. Eventually, it came to mean any opening in a ship's side, whether for cannon or not.

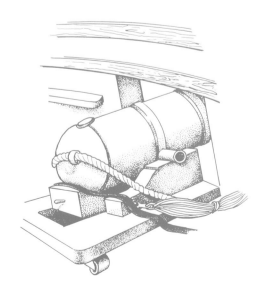

Picture-Painting Quotations

ERIC J. BERRYMAN, PH.D.

WHEN SOMETHING HISTORICAL and extraordinary happens, especially when men under arms achieve great deeds, ordinary human reaction first asks, "What happened?" and then wants to know, "What was said?"

In a fundamental and popular fashion we mark the progress of national aspirations, successes, or traumas by memorizing famous lines. America's presidents are perhaps as often remembered for what they said as for what they accomplished. Who does not associate a hearty "Bully!" with Teddy Roosevelt, champion of the great White Fleet, or remember that "a date which will live in infamy" marks former Assistant Secretary of the Navy FDR's response to America's entry into World War II? Washington, Jefferson, or Lincoln are probably as inspirational in modern times as they were in their own day. And not all words need to be associated with epic events in order to earn a niche in the historical memory. With a would-be assassin's bullet lodged about an inch away from his heart, former silver-screen hero Ronald Reagan's quip to his wife, "Honey, I forgot to duck," agrees soundly with Ernest Hemingway's definition that courage is, "grace under pressure."

In the U.S. Navy, words associated with historic deeds form part of the traditions that continue to inspire officers and crew in their duty. Established on October 13, 1775, "in Defense of Rights and Liberties," the Navy has been in the vanguard of every struggle or threat that this nation has confronted. With two mighty oceans flanking the continent—Great Lakes to the north and the formidable Gulf of Mexico to our south—the United States is frequently described as an island nation, and with the urgency of an island nation under siege we have always reached as far out as possible across blue waters whenever menaced by an adversary.

We strive to learn and remember the lessons history teaches us, and recall the words of a man like Themistocles who told his fellow Athenians some 2500 years ago, "Whosoever can hold the sea has command of everything." Our forward naval strategy—meet the enemy at his back door, not at yours—is traced to the time when Themistocles built up his fleet from 70 to 200 triremes (great wooden ships, powered by huge oars), just in time to save his country from invasion by Xerxes, king of Persia. "Your ships," he told his fellow Greeks, "are the wooden walls." It is a wonderfully old-fashioned analogy still true today: our modern ships can be described as latter day steel walls protecting the nation.

During the Revolutionary War, Admiral the Comte de Grasse blockaded the James and York rivers, and effected a strategic defeat of the British fleet under Admiral Howe at the Battle of the Chesapeake, thereby contributing decisively to Cornwallis' surrender at Yorktown, in 1781. This naval feat brilliantly illustrates George Washington's belief, in a letter to General Lafayette, that, "Without a decisive naval force, we can do nothing definitive. And with it, everything honourable and glorious." No doubt Washington had read his Themistocles. And very likely, so had Admiral Howe.

The American Revolution brought its own lexicon of immortal words to our naval fighting history. On the night of September 23, 1779, drifting between Filey Brig and Flamborough Head off the northeast coast of England, a newly built *HMS Serapis* was locked in death

Dr. ERIC J. BERRYMAN is a commander in the U.S. Reserve and a member of the National Maritime Historical Society of New York. He is director of the speakers bureau in the Navy Department's Office of Information.

Aboard *Bonhomme Richard*, John Paul Jones defeated the superior British frigate *Serapis*. During this famous battle, Jones cried, "I have not yet begun to fight!"

with the Continental Navy's *Bonhomme Richard*, an old French merchant ship recently converted into a warship, Captain John Paul Jones, Commanding.

The Royal Navy's Captain Richard Pearson had caused his ship's flag to be nailed to the sign that he would never surrender. When it seemed clear that victory over the American was the only outcome, so the story goes, he shouted across to Jones, "Has your ship struck?"

The reply, "I have not yet begun to fight," is the most well-known in U.S. Navy annals and embodies the very spirit of resistance even in the face of seemingly overwhelming opposition. Captain Pearson was eventually forced to tear down the English flag with his own hands. Despite all efforts by Jones and his crew, the *Bonhomme Richard's* battle damage was so great that she sank the next day.

In a letter to le Ray de Chaumont in November, 1778, Jones gave notice of his will to win, and of the indomitable fighting spirit American sailors have as their tradition: "I wish to have no connection with any ship that does not sail *fast*, for I intend *to go in harm's way*." Today, John Paul Jones' body rests in his tomb in the rotunda of a crypt at the U.S. Naval Academy, Annapolis, Maryland.

Bravery is a hallmark of our fledgling Navy during the Revolutionary War, when the ethic of uncompromising defiance was born. James Mugford's last words as his ship, the schooner *Franklin*, was being attacked in Boston Harbor in 1776 were, "Don't give up the vessel! You will be able to beat them off!" That this situation appeared hopeless was not the critical issue either to him or to his contemporaries; it was resistance in support of a great cause that mattered. Years later when freedom was again threatened and liberty put to the test, Captain James Lawrence may have remembered Mugford's words when he, too, lay wounded and dying. In the action between *USS Chesapeake* and *HMS Shannon*, June 1, 1813, Lawrence's last direction was, "Tell the men to fire faster and not give up the ship. Fight her till she sinks." It was the war of 1812, when the White House was burned and Independence lay in gave peril.

That war ratified our right to exist as a self-governing nation and it was won principally because we deployed some extraordinary ships, like *USS Constitution* and had the services of captains like Hull and Bainbridge and their extraordinary crews. Our resounding victories at sea established the U.S. Navy as a skillful and resolute force. Commodore Oliver Hazard Perry's report to General W. H. Harrison, September 10, 1813, underscores the ebullient spirits generated by the Navy's wins, "We have met the enemy and they are ours: two ships, two brigs, one schooner and one sloop."

Naval supremacy contributed mightily to the North's success in the Civil War, and while commerce raiders like *CSS Alabama* bedevilled Yankee merchant shipping, victory went to the side that mastered access to the open ocean. An order delivered in those days by Admiral David Glasgow Farragut, during the Battle of Mobile Bay, has been added to our naval traditions. Upon entering a mine field, August 5, 1864, (floating mines were known as "torpedoes" at that time) the Admiral commanded his subordinates, "Damn the torpedoes! Captain Drayton, go ahead! Jouett, full speed!" For his brilliance and daring in this battle and for other victories during the Civil War, the ranks of vice admiral and admiral were created to honor Farragut.

Humorous alliteration is no bar to memorable quotations, in fact it can be an effective means of dissolving tension. During the early, dark days of World War II, not long after Pearl Harbor, the Germans were

launching new submarines at the astonishing rate of 200 per year. As more U-boats went into action, the tonnage of British merchant shipping sunk rose alarmingly, to a peak of 650,000 tons a month. It was against that backdrop that Navy enlisted pilot, Aviation Machinist's Mate First Class Donald Mason, on anti-submarine patrol in the Atlantic, is credited with sending this message to his superiors: "Sighted sub. Sank same." The date was January 8, 1942. Those words rallied our Navy, our Armed Forces and the American public. Historical documents show that young Donald Mason hadn't sunk the reported submarine that day, but he *was* credited with a "kill" three months later, was promoted to Ensign and eventually advanced to the rank of Lieutenant before retirement.

The war was one of unprecedented bloodshed and fury, unrivalled in human history, and American ships and men were committed in epic numbers. Of destroyers and destroyer escorts alone, 25 were lost in the Atlantic and 57 were lost in the Pacific. Fiery courage and great loss of ships and personnel mark our way to victory in World War II, and no action symbolizes the spirit of the Naval Service more truly than the U.S. Marine Corps battle for Iwo Jima. In a Pacific Fleet communique,

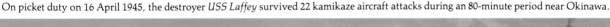

On picket duty on 16 April 1945, the destroyer *USS Laffey* survived 22 kamikaze aircraft attacks during an 80-minute period near Okinawa.

March 17, 1945, Fleet Admiral Chester Nimitz wrote, "Among the Americans who fought on Iwo Island, uncommon valor was a common virtue."

New eras also bring with them memorable words, as in 1955 when Eugene P. Wilkinson, Commanding Officer of the world's first operational nuclear submarine, *USS Nautilus*, sent his first official message, "Underway on nuclear power." And reaching to the stars and beyond the stars an eloquent naval aviator in 1969 told the world of his first progress on the moon, "That's one small step for a man, one giant leap for mankind." Neil A. Armstrong started his career learning about ships and the sea, and about the men and women without whom there would be no Navy and no tradition to honor.

Former Secretary of the Navy Paul H. Nitze commented that, "The sea is an unnatural environment for man, and it takes something extra for men to live with it." That special quality has contributed to a fine Navy, to our freedom as a nation and it continues to add to all of the splendid traditions embodied here, in the American seaman memorialized as the Lone Sailor.

J. William Middendorf, II, an Ambassador and Secretary of the Navy during our Bicentennial celebrations got to the heart of the matter when he said, "For 200 years the men and women of the United States Navy have served our nation significantly in peace and spectacularly in war." And a gallant ex-PT Boat skipper, John F. Kennedy, was absolutely on target when he addressed a group of brand new sailors, "Any man who may be asked in this century what he did to make his life worthwhile, I think can respond with a good deal of pride and satisfaction, 'I served in the United States Navy.' "

The nuclear-powered submarine *USS Billfish (Sturgeon* Class) surfaces at the North Pole during an exercise.

Navy Families Are Invaluable

Alice Stratton

Deputy Assistant Secretary of the Navy
for Personnel and Family Matters

The guided missile destroyer *USS Kidd* was preparing to deploy in several weeks to the Mediterranean from its homeport of Norfolk, Virginia. Husbands and wives met to talk about separations. The young couples sat holding hands, their arms around each other. Questions were raised. She was worried about his safety, and if he would continue to love her until they could be together again? Could she manage successfully, all the household chores, unexpected breakdown of appliances, the incredible loneliness and sense of loss? He felt guilty because he was excited to be going to sea, but also depressed because he was leaving his wife with all those responsibilities.

Fear of the unknown, depression, emotional withdrawal, unease about whether the marital bond was sturdy enough to withstand those long months of being apart . . . these were the concerns of the sailors and their wives.

The impact of long separations on devoted families of seafaring cultures has been legendary, from Homer's account of Penelope's fidelity to Odysseus during his 20-year cruise, down through the ages to modern times with Vice Admiral James Stockdale's eight-year ordeal as a POW in Vietnam. Family separation is nothing new to seafaring families whose lives are built around deployments. For as long as men have gone to sea, there have been loved ones left behind to carry on life as usual until the ship returned. In the old seaports along the northeast coast there are 19th century houses with

widow's walks perched high on the roof. From these heights, sea captains' wives would scan the horizon, hoping to get the first glimpse of their husband's returning ships. The sailors also missed their families, as shown by the intricately-carved and etched scrimshaw gifts they crafted during their time at sea. The strong Navy family support system has always been an integral part of how the sailors coped with life in that hostile environment. Almost without exception, those men who have been prisoners of war will tell you that one of the strongest influences on their ability to survive was the knowledge that they had a family waiting for them to return—and needing them to return.

> "Tell me, I'll forget
> Show me, I may remember
> But involve me, and I'll understand."
>
> —an old Chinese proverb

One of the keys to a strong Navy is the support of Navy families . . . and the most important way to gain family support is through an active, involved information program. It's no secret that families are the Navy's most important public—having a critical impact on retention and morale. Navy leaders recognized this long ago and they continually strive to improve communication at all levels, and through a variety of channels. Below are just some of the ways Navy commands communicate with families. One cannot place too high a value on this communication because behind almost every successful Navy person is an informed, supportive family.

■ *Dependents Cruise.* One of the best ways to inform is through first-hand experience. These cruises give

---

Alice Stratton is a real advocate. She's been there both professionally and personally. A licensed clinical social worker, a Navy wife whose husband was a Prisoner of War for many, many years, and a Navy/Marine mother and mother-in-law, she brings credibility and energy to her work.

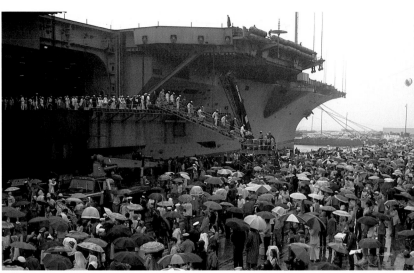

families a chance to see where mom or dad works and what jobs they perform.

■ *Sponsor Program.* Each newly assigned Navy man or woman is assigned a command sponsor to help the family get settled in the area.

■ *Telephone Tree.* Often headed by the wife of the commanding officer, this informal network of officer and enlisted wives is designed to pass along important information quickly. For instance, last-minute changes to the ship's operating schedule would pose no great problem if families could be contacted quickly and efficiently.

■ *Wives' Ombudsman.* A direct link between wives and the commanding officer to deal with dependent problems.

■ *Familygram.* A relaxed, conversational, personal message from the commanding officer to families, chock-full of useful information. Family communication is most critical in the case of deployed units, but stateside commands, ashore and afloat, also publish familygrams. Commanding officers can't be parents to all crewmembers and their families, but the familygram can help their parents and families rest easier at night.

■ *Videogram.* An extension of the familygram, this communications tool is fantastic for commands having access to videotape production and playback facilities. Mail call is valuable, but seeing and hearing your spouse and children while deployed gives a tremendous boost.

■ *CO's Welcome Aboard Letter.* A personal letter from the commanding officer to the newly reporting Navy

USS America and *USS Nimitz* appear as sleeping giants at dawn, Pier 12, Norfolk, Virginia.

man or woman. The letter should include a welcome to the family plus the names and phone numbers of the command sponsor and ombudsman.

- *CO's Action Line.* To establish two-way communication, this vehicle uses the ombudsman, familygram or the ship or station newspaper to allow and encourage dependents to ask questions and express opinions.

- *Emergency Assistance Procedures.* Dependents should be aware of the assistance that Navy Relief, the American Red Cross, the United Services Organization, the Armed Forces YMCA and the Navy Family Service Center can provide during personal emergencies. They should also know how to send a "Class Easy" message to their spouse via Western Union or through any Naval communications facility.

- *Wives' Clubs.* Every command should have active officer and enlisted wives' clubs. Command interest and sponsorship are often required to get the clubs started.

- *Dependents' School Tours.* Invite dependent children to bring their classmates for a tour of the command, and encourage them to establish a "pen pal" relationship with the ship's crew.

Although in the not-too-distant past the general Navy attitude seemed to be "If we had wanted sailors to have a family we would have issued them one," matters have definitely changed. For example, one of Navy's recruiting advertisements is aimed at families. The ad states, "We ask a lot from Navy families, and we try to give a lot back. Navy wife: It's the toughest job in the Navy." Several recent studies have shown that family considerations play a large and increasing role in determining the operational readiness of the Navy. The number one reason people leave the Navy is the long separations from the family required by extended sea duty.

Although civilian families also experience moves and tensions, Navy life differs in the frequency and intensity of these disruptions. No other occupation places as many stresses on the family.

Battleship *USS Iowa* in New York Harbor...soon to be her new homeport.

Heading the list of stresses are frequent and long deployments of ships, aviation squadrons and other units. During these separations, the Navy spouse is left to keep things running, becoming a single parent for all practical purposes, if there are children involved. On any given day, the Navy creates more than 84,000 single parent families through deployment. The parent who is away misses many special family events, such as holidays, anniversaries, birthdays, and all too often, the birth of a child.

Other stresses include frequent moves, with broken-off friendships, employment, school disruptions, participation in community organizations, inability to establish roots, cultural isolation overseas, overt or covert discrimination by the surrounding population, the ever-present threat of capture, injury or death during a mission, financial burdens created by short-fused, forced moves entailing the sale of a house, a lack of availability of adequate housing, etc.

A warm smile and an "I Love You" balloon welcome a sailor home from the sea.

Despite this stress and hardship, the Navy continues to attract high-caliber recruits and retain highly-skilled, motivated and experienced men and women. People who are proud to serve, justifiably proud of their accomplishments, and who accept the loneliness, thrive on hard work and who tolerate the isolation from family graciously.

The Navy recognizes the benefits of paying attention to the family. As one Navy officer recently told the New York Times, "We enlist sailors, but we re-enlist families."

In September 1985, the Department of the Navy established the Office of the deputy Assistant Secretary of the Navy for Personnel and Family Matters. This office was created to provide strong central oversight and coordination of program areas which affect the quality of life of Navy and Marine Corps service members and their families. For the first time, there is a specifically designated advocate for family programs at the highest policy levels of the Navy.

Navy Family Service Centers assist single and married personnel and their families with a variety of personal support services. An outgrowth of the 1978 Norfolk Family Awareness Conference, there are now 72 Family Service Centers around the world. The purpose of that original conference was to determine how the Navy could be more responsive to the unique needs and concerns of Navy families, and to identify the primary quality-of-life issues impacting Navy families.

Family Service Centers work hand-in-glove with other organizations in times of disaster. Response to the guided missile frigate USS Stark tragedy was awesome. The nation learned midday on a Sunday that the ship had been struck by an Exocet missile and men had been killed. In her homeport of Mayport, Florida, the Navy's support systems sprang into action to assist USS Stark families around the clock. The local Family Service Center contacted the ship's families who gathered together first at the ombudsman's home, and later at the on-base community center. Chaplains and social workers remained with the families through the interminable hours while waiting to learn who died and who survived. Wives clubs from other commands

The body of Navy diver Robert Stethem returns to Andrews Air Force Base from Beirut, where he was murdered by hijackers of TWA flight 847.

provided food; the Navy Relief society ensured emergency financial needs were met; airlines donated tickets to unite families; and the entire base and surrounding community reached out to protect and support the families whose husbands and fathers and sons, nephews and uncles, grandfathers and grandsons had fallen in harm's way.

It is that inner strength and built-in support system that makes and keeps the Navy family strong, responsive and capable of dealing with misfortune.

A decade ago, family support was a collateral duty for staff corps and voluntary agencies supporting the commanding officer and his division officers. Now the Family Service Center and a network of other support organizations provide assistance not only when his ship or squadron is in homeport but, more importantly, while it is deployed. These centers have quickly become a key part of Navy life. A ship's commanding officer, reflecting a widespread view, unequivocally stated: "The family service centers and ombudsman are the heart and nerves of this command. I don't know how we would have managed through the last deployment without the help of these wonderful people."

A strong national defense depends on strong military families. The military must be committed to the family in order to get the best from its service members. Today's Navy and Marine Corps have that commitment. Sir Basil Liddell Hart, the British military historian, summed it all up very well when he wrote: "Man has two supreme loyalties—to country and to family. So long as their families are safe, they will defend their country, believing that by their sacrifice they are safeguarding their families also. But even the bonds of patriotism, discipline and comradeship are loosened when the family is threatened."

The fiber binding together members of today's Navy family has never been stronger. Reenlistment figures are at an all-time high. Morale amongst sailors has never been better. We have a healthy, effective Navy comprised of intelligent, committed professionals who work hard enthusiastically, knowing that they have the full support of their spouses, children, parents, and friends and the respect of a grateful nation. ⌐╤

EDITOR'S NOTE: *Dr. Alice Ivey Snyder, Deputy Director, Norfolk Navy Family Services Center, contributed significantly to this chapter.*

Stripes and Stars Forever

Secretaries of the Navy

Benjamin Stoddert
Jun 1798—Mar 1801

Robert Smith
Jul 1801—Mar 1809

Paul Hamilton
May 1809—Dec 1812

William Jones
Jan 1813—Dec 1814

B. W. Crowninshield
Jan 1815—Sep 1818

Smith Thompson
Jan 1819—Aug 1823

Samuel Southard
Sep 1823—Mar 1829

John Branch
Mar 1829—Mar 1831

Levi Woodbury
May 1831—Jun 1834

Mahlen Dickerson
Jul 1834—Jun 1838

James K. Paulding
Jul 1838—Mar 1841

George E. Badger
Mar 1841—Sep 1841

Abel P. Upshur
Oct 1841— Jul 1843

David Henshaw
Jul 1843—Feb 1844

Thomas W. Gilmer
Feb 1844—Feb 1844

John Y. Mason
Mar 1844—Mar 1845

George Bancroft
Mar 1845—Sep 1846

John Y. Mason
Sep 1846—Mar 1849

William B. Preston
Mar 1849—Jul 1850

William A. Graham
Aug 1850—Jul 1852

John P. Kennedy
Jul 1852—Mar 1853

James C. Dobbin
Mar 1853—Mar 1857

Isaac Toucey
Mar 1857—Mar 1861

Gideon Welles
Mar 1861—Mar 1869

Adolph E. Borie
Mar 1869—Jun 1869

George N. Robeson
Jun 1869—Mar 1877

Richard W. Thompson
Mar 1877—Dec 1880

Nathan Goff, Jr.
Jan 1881—Mar 1881

William H. Hunt
Mar 1881—Apr 1882

William E. Chandler
Apr 1882—Mar 1885

William C. Whitney
Mar 1885—Mar 1889

Benjamin F. Tracy
Mar 1889—Mar 1893

Hilary A. Herbert
Mar 1893—Mar 1897

John D. Long
Mar 1897—Apr 1902

William H. Moody
May 1902—Jun 1904

Paul Morton
Jul 1904—Jun 1905

C. J. Bonaparte
Jul 1905—Dec 1906

Victor R. Metcalf
Dec 1906—Nov 1908

Truman H. Newberry
Dec 1908—Mar 1909

George von L. Meyer
Mar 1909—Mar 1913

Joesphus Daniels
Mar 1913—Mar 1921

Edwin Denby
Mar 1921—Mar 1924

Curtis Wilbur
Mar 1924—Mar 1929

Charles F. Adams
Mar 1929—Mar 1933

Claude A. Swanson
Mar 1933—Jul 1939

Charles Edison
Jan 1940—Jun 1940

Frank Knox
Jul 1940—Apr 1944

James Forrestal
May 1944—Sep 1947

John L. Sullivan
Sep 1947—May 1949

Francis P. Matthews
May 1949—Jul 1951

Dan A. Kimball
Jul 1951—Jan 1953

Robert B. Anderson
Feb 1953—May 1954

Charles S. Thomas
May 1954—Mar 1957

Thomas S. Gates, Jr.
Apr 1957—Jun 1959

William B. Franke
Jun 1959—Jan 1961

John B. Connally
Jan 1961—Dec 1961

Fred Korth
Jan 1962—Nov 1963

Paul H. Nitze
Nov 1963—Jun 1967

Paul R. Ignatius
Sep 1967—Jan 1969

John H. Chaffee
Jan 1969—May 1972

John Warner
May 1972—Apr 1974

J. William Middendorf II
Jun 1974—Jan 1977

W. Graham Claytor
Feb 1977—Aug 1979

Edward Hidalgo
Oct 1979—Jan 1981

John Lehman
Feb 1981—Apr 1987

James H. Webb, Jr.
Apr 1987—Present

Chiefs of Naval Operations

Admiral William S. Benson
May 1915—Sep 1919

Admiral Robert E. Coontz
Nov 1919—Jul 1923

Admiral Edward W. Eberle
Jul 1923—Nov 1927

Admiral Charles F. Hughes
Nov 1927—Sep 1929

Admiral William V. Pratt
Sep 1929—Jun 1933

Admiral William H. Standley
Jul 1933—Jan 1937

Admiral William D. Leahy
Jan 1939—Aug 1939

Admiral Harold R. Stark
Aug 1939—Mar 1942

Admiral Ernest J. King
Mar 1942—Dec 1945

Fleet Admiral Chester W. Nimitz
Dec 1945—Dec 1947

Admiral Louis E. Denfeld
Dec 1947—Nov 1949

Admiral Forrest P. Sherman
Nov 1949—Nov 1951

Admiral William M. Fechteler
Aug 1951—Aug 1953

Admiral Robert B. Carney
Aug 1953—Aug 1955

Admiral Arleigh A. Burke
Aug 1955—Aug 1961

Admiral George W. Anderson
Aug 1961—Aug 1963

Admiral David L. McDonald
Aug 1963—Aug 1967

Admiral Thomas H. Moorer
Aug 1967—Jul 1970

Admiral Elmo R. Zumwalt, Jr.
Jul 1970—Jul 1974

Admiral James L. Holloway III
Jul 1974—Jul 1978

Admiral Thomas B. Hayward
Jul 1978—Jul 1982

Admiral James D. Watkins
Jul 1982—Jun 1986

Admiral Carlisle A. H. Trost
Jul 1986—Present

Master Chief Petty Officers of the Navy

GMCM Delbert D. Black
Jan 1967—Apr 1971

MACM John D. Whittet
Apr 1971—Sep 1975

OSCM Robert J. Walker
Sep 1975—Sep 1979

AFCM Thomas S. Crow
Sep 1979—Oct 1982

AVCM Billy C. Sanders
Oct 1982—Oct 1985

RMCM (SW) William H. Plackett
Oct 1985—Present

A copy of the original Union Jack flown in the Continental Navy, first hoisted on December 3, 1775.

DONT TREAD ON ME

United States Navy Memorial Foundation Contributions/Pledges

Fleet Organization

Fleet Commanders in Chief
($500,000 and over)
Fleet Reserve Association

Fleet Commanders
($250,000 and over)
Grumman Corporation

Task Force Commanders
($200,000 and over)
General Dynamics Corporation
General Electric Company
Lockheed Corporation

Task Group Commanders
($150,000 and over)
Boeing Company
Japanese Maritime Self-Defense Force
 and Civilian Volunteers
Martin Marietta Corporation
McDonnell Douglas Corporation
Rockwell International
Texaco Inc.
Unisys Corporation

Flotilla Commanders
($100,000 and over)
Government of Argentina
Government of Australia
Government of France
Government of the Republic of China
Government of the Republic of Korea
Government of Spain
Jacksonville Navy Memorial Foundation,
 Inc.
Raytheon Company
United Technologies Corporation

Squadron Commanders
($50,000 and over)
Avenue Associates, Trammell Crow Co.,
 Dutch Institutional Holding Co.
Babcock & Wilcox Company
Mrs. Robert Crown
Destroyer Escort Sailors Association
General Motors Corporation
Goodyear Tire and Rubber Company
Gould Inc.
Hughes Aircraft Company
GMC John Kopach, USN (Ret.)
Ladies Auxiliary of the FRA
Naval Order of the United States
System Planning Corporation
Textron
Women in the Navy

Division Commanders
($25,000 and over)
Allied-Signal Inc.
Bloedorn Foundation
British Aerospace, Inc.
Eaton Corporation
Mr. and Mrs. Zachary Fisher
Norfolk Southern Corporation
Northrop Corporation
Quadrangle Development Corporation
Sanders Associates, Inc.
W. M. Schlosser, Co.
U.S. Naval Institute Foundation

Unit Commanders
($10,000 and over)
AFL-CIO
Amerada Hess Corporation
American Electric Power Company
American Express Company
American Petroleum Institute
Ashland Oil Foundation
Bath Iron Works
Brown Foundation, Inc.
Mr. and Mrs. C. Thomas Clagett, Jr.
D.C. Council, Navy League
 of the United States
Emerson Electric Company
E-Systems, Inc.
Freed Foundation
Grand Hyatt Washington
S. Steven Karalekas
Kirby Foundation
RCA Corporation
Samuel Wm. Sax
Scientific Management Associates, Inc.
Shell Companies Foundation
Tesoro Petroleum Corporation
Texas Instruments
TRW, Inc.

Ship Captains
($5,000 and over)
ANA Washington-Anacostia Squadron
Battle Group Delta
Berlin Publications, Inc.
Bird-Johnson Company
Booz Allen & Hamilton, Inc.
Captain and Mrs. Gordon H. Clow
Colt Industries Inc.
Delaware Investment Association

DynCorp
Eastman Kodak Company, Government
 Systems
Evaluation Research Corporation
Fansteel/Custom Technologies Corporation
Paul Fay
Federal Data Corporation
Figgie International
G.D. Searle & Co.
GEICO
Grabill Corporation
Charles Hajcsisak
Paul N. Howell
Howell Corporation
Indal Limited
Kirkpatrick Foundation, Inc.
Kollsman Instrument Company
Kretschmar Brands, Inc.
Litton Industries
Maersk Line, Limited
National Steel and Shipbuilding Company
Naval Air Facility, Atsugi
Navistar
Newport News Shipbuilding
 and Dry Dock Co.
Mr. and Mrs. Phillip G. Norton
ORI Group
Pagliaro Brothers Stone Co., Inc.
B. Waring Partridge
Peterson Builders, Inc.
Philip Morris Companies, Inc.
Mrs. W. C. Reeder
Mrs. Eugene Henry Rietzke
Rolls-Royce Inc.
Sippican Inc.
Sparton Corproration
Mr. and Mrs. Roger Staubach
Marvin Stone
Syscon Corporation
Todd Shipyards, Inc.
United Services Life Insurance Company
United States Historical Society
U.S. Naval Academy Alumni Association
U.S. Submarine Veterans of World War II
Veda International, Inc.
Virginia Power Company
Vitro Corporation
VSE Corporation
Whitehead Foundation
Williams International

Pledges as of October 1987

Navy Memorial Support

THE FOLLOWING COMPANIES have contributed $1,000 toward publishing the Navy Memorial Commemorative Book:

Advanced Marine Enterprises, Inc.
Analysis & Technology, Inc.
Arthur Andersen & Co.
AT&T Federal Systems
The Boeing Company
Communications Satellite Corp. (COMSAT)
Control Data Corporation
District of Columbia Council Navy League
Eastman Kodak Company, Gov't Systems
EDO Corporation
Electronic Data Systems Corp. (EDS)
Emerson Electric Company
GEICO and Affiliates
Harris Corporation
Hewlett Packard Company
Honeywell, Inc.
Hughes Aircraft Company
Lucas Aerospace Inc.
Magnavox Gov't & Electronics Co.
Martin Marietta Corp.
Morrison Knudsen Corp.
National Security Industrial Assn.
Newport News Shipbuilding
Sea-Land Corporation
Sundstrand Corporation
United Services Automobile Assoc.
United Technologies Corporation
United Technologies, Norden Systems
VEDA International Inc.

THE BOARD OF DIRECTORS AND STAFF of the U.S. Navy Memorial Foundation are indebted to many individuals and companies that have contributed to the overall success of the planning, construction and dedication of the U.S. Navy Memorial. We thank each of them for their support and express special appreciation to:

Pennsylvania Avenue Development Corporation
Office of the Mayor, Washington, D.C.
Department of the Interior
National Archives
Commission of Fine Arts
National Capital Planning Commission
Department of the Navy
Defense Mapping Service
W.M. Schlosser Co., Inc.
Pagliaro Brothers Stone Co.
New England Stone, Inc.
Columbia Welders and Iron Works, Inc.
Central Armature Works
Gilbane Building Co./
   Paul R. Jackson Construction Co.
Conklin Rossant Architects
Wheaton Van Lines, Inc.
Columbia Gardens Memorials
Iwerks Entertainment
McGillivray Freeman Productions
Robert F. Jani Productions
Fleet Reserve Association
Ladies Auxiliary
   of the Fleet Reserve Association
Dahlgren Division, Naval Sea Cadets
Maryland Sound
National Capital Flag Co., Inc.
Flag Heritage Foundation
Interspace Design Group
John J. Christie & Associates
Lynch Industries

United States Navy Memorial Foundation

Staff

RADM William Thompson, USN (Ret.)
President

CAPT Robert S. Jones, USN (Ret.)
Executive Assistant

Mrs. B.J. Andrews
Mrs. Stevii Graves
Paul Haley
CAPT. G. H. McLeod, USN (Ret.)
Mrs. Hope McLeod
CDR J. J. Nemer, USN (Ret.)
Miss Nicole Peters
Master Chief Lana Tobey, USN (Ret.)

Former Staff Members

Mrs. Ruth Donohue
CAPT John R. Davey, USN (Ret.)
Miss Karen DuBois
Miss Stefanie Graves
Mrs. Sally Jurkowsky
Chief Marcy Nevarez, USN (Ret.)
CAPT Walter "R" Thomas, USN (Ret.)
Brian Thompson
Miss Zoe Wages
Mrs. Dorothy Thompson, Mrs. Lucy Roxbury, Mrs. June Mayo, Mrs. Doris Hatfield, Mrs. Lois Brown, and the many other *volunteers* who have donated time and effort to the building of the Memorial.

Ship Associations and Veterans Groups

THE FOLLOWING SHIP REUNION GROUPS AND ASSOCIATIONS responded to an open invitation to send a representative to the United States Navy Memorial Dedication Ceremony who would carry a banner bearing the group's name in a ceremonial procession:

USS Woolsey (DD 437)
USS Corry (DD 463)
USS Henrico (APA 45)
USS Balch (DD 363)
USS Porterfield (DD 682)
USS Biloxi (CL 80)
USS Franks (DD 554)
USS Pittsburgh (CA 72)
USS Fletcher (DD 445)
USS Quillback (SS 424)
USS Amsterdam (CL 101)
USS Kephart (APD 61)
USS Stockton (DD 646)
USS President Adams (APA 19)
USS Phelps (DD 360)
USS Phoenix (CL 46)
USS LST-312
USS Saint Paul (CA 73)
USS Princeton (CVL 23)
USS Northampton (CA 26)
USS Thatcher (DD 514)
USS Charles Ausburne (DD 570)
USS Ellyson (DD 454/DMS 19)
USS Consolation (AH 15)
USS Lang (DD 399)
USS Converse (DD 509)
USS LST-602
USS South Dakota (BB 57)
USS Dyson (DD 572)
USS Yosemite (AD 19)
USS Whitehurst (DE 634)
USS Spence (DD 512)
USS Callaghan (DD 792)
USS Salt Lake City (CL 25)
USS Lexington (CV 16)
USS Houston (CA 30/CL 81)
USS Aulick (DD 569)
USS Ammen (DD 527)
USS Register (APD 92)
USS Nashville (CL 43)
USS Wadsworth (DD 516)
USS Wharton (AP 7)
USS Shangri-La (CVA 38)
USS William Seiverling (DE 441)
USS Reno (CL 96)
USS Hamilton (DMS 18)
USS Topeka (CL 67)
USS Mustin (DD 413)
USS Melvin (DD 680

USS Walter B. Cobb (APD 106)
USS Ingersoll (DD 652)
USS Rinehart (DE 196)
USS Wickes (DD 578)
USS Enterprise (CV 6)
USS LST-389
USS Foote (DD 511)
USS Patterson (DD 392)
USS Washington (BB 56)
USS Ranger (CV 4)
USS Drexler (DD 741)
USS Blackfish (SS 221)
USS LST-508
USS Indiana
USS Gwin (DD 433)
USS Copahee (CVE 12/VGS 12)
Pearl Harbor
   Survivors Association, Inc.
Non-Commissioned Officers
   Association of the USA
Naval Research Association
Gold Star Wives of America
Reserve Officers Association
   of the United States
Jewish War Veterans of the USA
The American Legion
United States LST Association
The Little Beavers, DesRon 23
USN Armed Guard, World War II
Scouting Squadron Fifty-Five (VS-55)
Pearl Harbor History Associates
Peter Tare, Inc.
Naval Cryptologic Veterans
U.S. Submarine Veterans, World War II
Utility Squadron Two (VJ-2)
Tin Can Sailors
Chesapeake Unit, Waves National
U.S. Armed Guard of Florida
P.T. Boaters of World War II
Garden State Chapter,
   Destroyer Escort Sailors Assn.
Naval Mine Warfare Association
Patrol Craft Sailors Association
Air Group 16
Navy Women's Association
Destroyer Escort Sailors Assoc.
Armed Services YMCA

U.S. Navy Memorial Dedication Committee

John P. Cosgrove, Chairman
Paul C. Miller
Captain George Seaboo, USNR, (Ret.)
Paul T. Haley
Tom Coldwell

Special Assistants
Anne Hartzell, Pennsylvania Avenue
   Development Corp.
Commander Tom Connor, U.S. Navy
Lieutenant Leo Leary, U.S. Navy
Lieutenant Nettie Johnson, U.S. Navy
Dr. Frank G. Burke, U.S. Archives

U.S. Navy Memorial Dedication Ceremony created by Robert F. Jani Productions, Inc.

About the Editor

JOHN W. ALEXANDER was born on October 21, 1947 in Coral Gables, Florida. He grew up in southern Florida, attended Florida State University and in 1971, on a Naval ROTC full scholarship, graduated from the University of Missouri with an MA in Journalism.

That same year, he received a commission in the U.S. Navy and embarked on a career that has included assignments as anti-submarine warfare officer aboard two destroyers and navigator aboard a guided missile destroyer. Next, focusing on an interest in public affairs, his assignments took him to Norfolk, New York City and Washington, D.C. He coordinated media operations for the Fifth International Naval Review, conducted in support of the Statue of Liberty Centennial celebration, coordinating requests for accreditation from more than 5,000 international news media representatives. He is currently assigned to the Pentagon as Director of Field Operations in the Office of the Chief of Information.

This is Commander Alexander's second book. "Liberty Centennial: The Fourth of July Weekend," was published in October 1986. He and his wife, Theresa Marie, live in Alexandria, Virginia, with their two children, Richard, 9, and Catherine, 3.

Flags That Talk

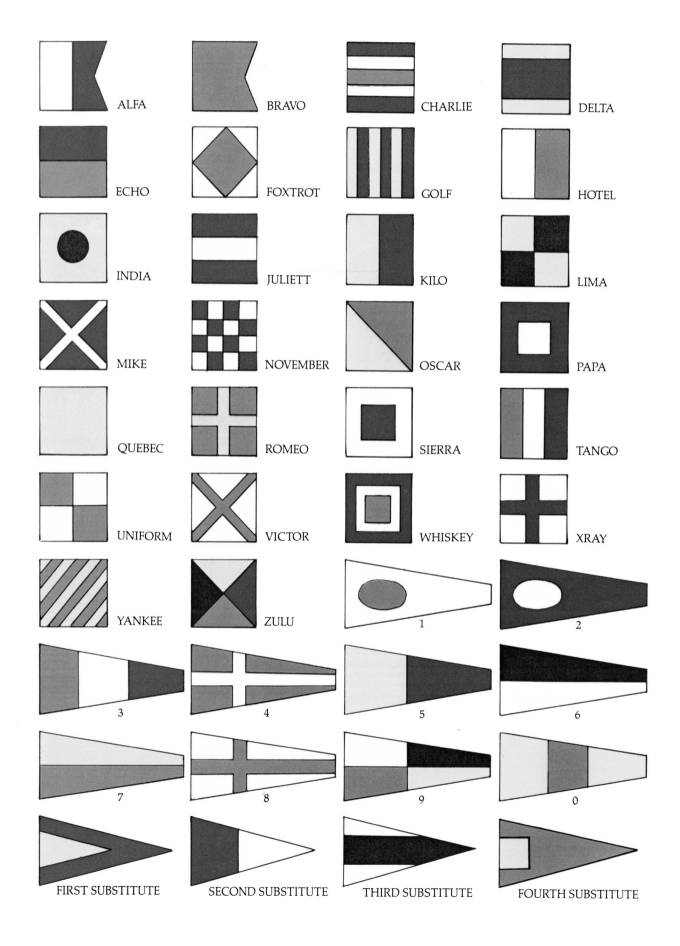

Photo Credits

JOCS Cindy Adams: 8, top 13, bottom right 18, bottom 19; CDR John W. Alexander: 176; PHC Edwin Bailey: 165; PHCS R.W. Bayles: 65; PH3 Tom Brewer: 14; Howard Chandler Christy: painting 159; Tom Coldwell: 43; PH2 Carl L. Duvall: 72, 80, top 135, 160; D.B. Eckard: 109; Russell Egnor: 7, top right 18, bottom 20, top 23, 77; PH1 R.A. Elder: 128, 131; Sharon Farmer: 170; Chuck Feil: 101; PH2 Michael D.P. Flynn: 56, bottom 61, top 64, bottom 69, 76, top and center 82, 83, 126, 136, top 139, 140, 175; PHC John Francavillo: 46; LT Emmett Francois: bottom right 73,110; PH1 Harold J. Gerwein: 6, top left 12, center 13, 15, top left 19, top 22, 54, 57, 62, top left and middle left 70,78, right center 84, bottom 86, bottom 162, center left, bottom right and above 163; PH3 Darryl Glubczynski: bottom 96; PH1 (AC) R.H. Green: 9; Gerald W. Grimm: 68; John Hamilton: paintings 124, 157; CWO4 Walt Hamler: bottom 139; PH1 (DV) R. Hasha: 102, 103; CDR Charles J. Heatley, III: 59, top 73; PH2 Thomas Hensley: 50; PH1 (SW) Jeff R. Hilton: 49, 52, bottom 84 bottom 85, top 87, 95, top 96, top 97, 154, top left 162; PH2 Carl H. Jackson, Sr.: 105; JO1 Lynn E. Jenkins: 116, 153; Robert Jones: left 22, bottom 23, 31-40; JOCS Fred J. Klinkenberger, Jr.: center 61, 114, 115, 167; John Landry: painting 93; PH2 T.P. McAuliffe: center 73; Ernest McIver: 164; K.J. Mierzejewski: 108; Tom Mitchell: painting 156; PHC Terry C. Mitchell: 48, 71; Edward Moran: painting 119; PH1 Chuck Mussi: top right and bottom 12, bottom 13, 16, bottom 17, left 18, top right and center right 19, top 20, 21, 24, 25, bottom 64, top 69, bottom left, top right and center right 70,99, bottom right 104, 132, 133, 137, bottom 138, 158, top right 162, bottom left 163; PHCS Ken Nichols: top 138; PHC Roy Ojala: bottom 97; Jon Ortner: 27, 81; PH2 Paul Pappas: top right 84, top 86, top 163, 166; PH1 Norman P. Plummer: 58; PH1 Jim Preston: 5; Sabella: 42; PH2 R. Sforza: bottom 87; PH2 Layne Smith: bottom 82; Pat Jett Toombs: top 17, center 20; R. Whitehead: painting 2; PH2 Judith L. Wilkinson: 66; PHC Harold Wise: bottom 135; Brian Wolff: 53, 60, top 85.

Additional thanks to Naval Imaging Command, Navy Archives, National Archives and the Memphis Council of the Navy League. Finally, Pat Jett Toombs was of invaluable assistance in providing photo research.

Sea Fever

I must go down to the seas again, to the lonely sea and sky,
and all I ask is a tall ship and a star to steer her by,
and the wheel's kick and the wind's song and the white sail's shaking,
and a gray mist on the sea's face and a gray dawn breaking.

I must go down to the seas again, for the call of the running tide
is a wild call and a clear call that may not be denied;
and all I ask is a windy day with the white clouds flying,
and the flung spray and the blown spume, and the seagulls crying.

I must go down to the seas again to the vagrant gypsy life,
to the gull's way and the whale's way where the wind's like a whetted knife;
and all I ask is a merry yarn from a laughing fellow rover,
and quiet sleep and a sweet dream when the long trick's over.

— John Masefield